Mastering The Markets: A Comprehensive Guide to Trading Psychology and Strategies

Dave Gaufrette

Published by All Trader's Hub, 2024.

While every precaution has been taken in the preparation of this book, the publisher assumes no responsibility for errors or omissions, or for damages resulting from the use of the information contained herein.

MASTERING THE MARKETS: A COMPREHENSIVE GUIDE TO TRADING PSYCHOLOGY AND STRATEGIES

First edition. March 2, 2024.

Copyright © 2024 Dave Gaufrette.

ISBN: 979-8224444977

Written by Dave Gaufrette.

Table of Contents

Mastering The Markets: A Comprehensive Guide to Trading Psychology and Strategies

By Dave Gaufrette

Preface

Welcome to "Mastering the Markets: A Comprehensive Guide to Trading Psychology and Strategies." In the fast-paced world of trading, success often hinges not just on technical analysis or market knowledge, but also on mastering the psychological aspects of trading and implementing effective strategies.

This ebook is designed to be your roadmap to navigating the complexities of trading psychology and strategies. Drawing from the insights of seven influential books, we've curated a collection of wisdom that covers everything from understanding market dynamics to developing a winning mindset and executing trades with precision.

Whether you're just starting your trading journey or looking to refine your skills, this ebook offers practical guidance that you can apply immediately. Each chapter is crafted to provide valuable insights and actionable strategies that will empower you to make better trading decisions and achieve your financial goals.

We believe that success in trading is not just about making profits, but also about mastering yourself and your approach to the markets. With dedication, discipline, and the right knowledge, you can unlock your full potential as a trader and thrive in today's dynamic market environment.

So, without further ado, let's dive into "Mastering the Markets" and embark on a journey to trading mastery together. Here's to your success in the exciting world of trading!

Introduction

Welcome to " Mastering The Markets: A Comprehensive Guide to Trading Psychology and Strategies." In this ebook, we'll delve into the intricate world of forex trading psychology and explore the most effective strategies to help you navigate the challenges and maximize your success in the forex market.

Forex trading is not just about analyzing charts and executing trades; it's also about mastering your own emotions and psychology. The ability to control your emotions, stay disciplined, and maintain a clear mindset is crucial for success in the highly volatile and fast-paced world of forex trading.

In this ebook, we'll cover various psychological principles, techniques, and strategies that traders can implement to improve their decision-making process, manage risk effectively, and ultimately enhance their overall trading performance.

Chapter 1: Understanding the Psychology of Forex Trading

The Crucial Role of Psychology in Forex Trading Success

In the fast-paced and volatile world of forex trading, success isn't solely determined by technical analysis, market knowledge, or trading strategies. A crucial yet often underestimated factor in achieving consistent profitability is the trader's psychology. The importance of psychology in forex trading cannot be overstated, as it influences every aspect of a trader's decision-making process, risk management, and overall performance.

Understanding Emotions:

Emotions play a significant role in forex trading, often driving traders to make impulsive decisions that deviate from their trading plans. Fear, greed, hope, and regret are among the most common emotions experienced by traders. Fear of missing out (FOMO) can lead traders to enter trades hastily, while fear of losing (FOLO) can prevent them from taking necessary risks. Greed can cause traders to hold onto winning positions for too long, while hope can keep them clinging to losing trades in the hope of a reversal. Regret over past losses or missed opportunities can cloud judgment and hinder future decision-making.

Impact on Decision-Making:

Psychological biases, such as confirmation bias and overconfidence, can distort traders' perceptions and lead to faulty decision-making. Confirmation bias causes traders to seek out information that confirms their existing beliefs while ignoring contradictory evidence, potentially leading to biased analysis and flawed trade setups. Overconfidence can make traders overly optimistic about their abilities, leading them to take excessive risks or neglect proper risk management practices. These biases can contribute to losses and prevent traders from objectively evaluating market conditions and adjusting their strategies accordingly.

Maintaining Discipline:

MASTERING THE MARKETS: A COMPREHENSIVE GUIDE TO TRADING PSYCHOLOGY AND STRATEGIES

Discipline is paramount in forex trading, as it enables traders to stick to their trading plans and avoid emotional decision-making. A disciplined trader follows a set of predefined rules for entering and exiting trades, managing risk, and allocating capital. This discipline helps mitigate the impact of emotions on trading decisions and ensures consistency in performance over time. Without discipline, traders are more likely to succumb to impulsive behavior, deviate from their strategies, and experience erratic results.

Managing Risk Effectively:

Psychology plays a crucial role in risk management, as it influences traders' willingness to take risks and their ability to accept losses. Fear of losing capital can cause traders to set overly tight stop-loss orders or avoid trades altogether, limiting their profit potential. On the other hand, overconfidence can lead traders to take excessive risks, risking large losses that can wipe out their accounts. Effective risk management requires a balance between risk and reward, as well as the ability to accept losses as part of the trading process without letting them negatively impact future decisions.

Developing a Winning Mindset:

Successful forex traders cultivate a winning mindset characterized by patience, resilience, and adaptability. They understand that trading is a marathon, not a sprint, and focus on long-term profitability rather than short-term gains. A winning mindset enables traders to maintain confidence in their abilities during periods of drawdowns and losses, as well as to learn from their mistakes and continuously improve their strategies. By developing mental toughness and emotional resilience, traders can navigate the challenges of forex trading with confidence and achieve their financial goals.

The importance of psychology in forex trading cannot be overstated. Emotions, biases, discipline, and mindset all play crucial roles in determining a trader's success or failure in the forex market. By understanding the psychological aspects of trading and actively working to cultivate a disciplined mindset, traders can enhance their decision-making process, manage risk effectively, and ultimately achieve consistent profitability in forex trading.

Navigating the Mind Game: Common Psychological Challenges Faced by Forex Traders

Forex trading, with its potential for high returns and rapid market movements, can be both exhilarating and daunting. While mastering the technical aspects of trading is essential, equally crucial is understanding and managing the psychological challenges that traders face. From battling emotions to coping with uncertainty, here are some common psychological hurdles encountered by forex traders:

1. Fear and Anxiety:

Fear is perhaps the most prevalent emotion experienced by forex traders. Fear of losing money, fear of missing out on profitable trades, and fear of making wrong decisions can paralyze traders and prevent them from executing trades according to their strategies. Anxiety often accompanies fear, leading to indecision and second-guessing, which can result in missed opportunities or poorly timed trades.

2. Greed and Overtrading:

On the flip side of fear lies greed, another potent psychological force that can sabotage trading success. The desire for quick profits or the temptation to recoup losses can drive traders to overtrade, deviating from their risk management plans and exposing themselves to unnecessary risk. Overtrading often leads to emotional exhaustion and impulsive decision-making, which can have detrimental effects on trading performance.

3. Impatience and FOMO:

In the world of forex trading, patience is indeed a virtue. However, many traders struggle with impatience, especially when faced with periods of slow market movement or consolidation. This impatience can lead traders to abandon their trading strategies in search of more action or to enter trades prematurely, ignoring key indicators or risk factors. Fear of missing out (FOMO) exacerbates this impatience, driving traders to chase after trending markets or enter trades without proper analysis, often with unfavorable outcomes.

4. Emotional Attachment to Trades:

It's natural for traders to become emotionally attached to their trades, particularly when they're winning or losing. Winning trades can fuel feelings of euphoria and overconfidence, leading traders to hold onto positions longer than they should or to increase position sizes excessively. Conversely, losing trades can trigger feelings of frustration, disappointment, or self-doubt, causing traders to hesitate in cutting their losses or to engage in revenge trading to recoup losses, further exacerbating the situation.

5. Confirmation Bias:

Confirmation bias is a cognitive bias that causes traders to seek out information that confirms their existing beliefs or biases while ignoring contradictory evidence. In forex trading, confirmation bias can manifest in various forms, such as selectively interpreting technical indicators or news events to fit a preconceived narrative or disregarding warning signs that suggest a change in market direction. This bias can cloud judgment and lead to poor decision-making, as traders fail to objectively assess market conditions or consider alternative viewpoints.

6. Lack of Discipline:

Discipline is the bedrock of successful forex trading, yet it's a challenge many traders struggle with. Without discipline, traders may deviate from their trading plans, abandon risk management principles, or succumb to impulsive behavior. Whether it's entering trades based on emotions rather than analysis, failing to adhere to stop-loss levels, or neglecting proper trade execution procedures, a lack of discipline can undermine even the most well-thought-out trading strategies.

MASTERING THE MARKETS: A COMPREHENSIVE GUIDE TO TRADING PSYCHOLOGY AND STRATEGIES

The psychological challenges faced by forex traders are diverse and ever-present, but they are not insurmountable. By recognizing these challenges and actively working to address them, traders can cultivate the mental resilience and emotional discipline needed to succeed in the dynamic world of forex trading. Whether through mindfulness techniques, journaling, or seeking support from mentors or trading communities, mastering the psychological aspects of trading is an essential step towards achieving long-term profitability and success.

Unveiling the Influence: The Role of Emotions in Trading

In the high-stakes arena of financial markets, where fortunes are made and lost in the blink of an eye, emotions play a pivotal role in shaping trading outcomes. From seasoned professionals to novice traders, everyone is susceptible to the powerful sway of emotions such as fear, greed, hope, regret, and even the vengeful urge. Understanding how these emotions influence trading decisions is key to mastering the art of successful trading.

1. Fear:

Fear is perhaps the most primal and pervasive emotion experienced by traders. Fear of losing money, fear of missing out on profitable opportunities, and fear of making wrong decisions can all paralyze traders and hinder their ability to execute trades with confidence. When fear takes hold, traders may hesitate to pull the trigger on trades, second-guess their analysis, or exit winning positions prematurely out of a fear of losing profits. Left unchecked, fear can lead to a cycle of avoidance and missed opportunities, ultimately undermining trading performance.

2. Greed:

Greed is the insatiable desire for more, often fueled by the allure of quick profits and the fear of missing out on lucrative opportunities. When greed takes over, traders may abandon rational risk management practices in pursuit of greater gains, increasing position sizes beyond prudent levels or holding onto winning trades for too long in the hope of even higher returns. However, unchecked greed can lead to overtrading, excessive risk-taking, and ultimately, substantial losses when the market inevitably turns against them.

3. Hope:

Hope is the optimistic belief that things will turn out for the best, even in the face of adversity. In trading, hope can be both a blessing and a curse. While a positive outlook can help traders maintain resilience in the face of losses and setbacks, excessive hope can cloud judgment and lead to irrational decision-making. Traders may hold onto losing positions in the hope of a reversal, ignoring warning signs and failing to cut their losses when necessary. Hope can prolong the agony of a losing streak and prevent traders from accepting reality and moving on to more promising opportunities.

4. Regret:

Regret is the emotional distress caused by the realization that one's actions or decisions have led to unfavorable outcomes. In trading, regret often stems from missed opportunities or poor decisions that result in losses. Traders may dwell on past mistakes, replaying scenarios in their minds and lamenting what could have been. Regret can erode confidence, breed self-doubt, and hinder future decision-making, as traders become paralyzed by the fear of repeating past errors. Learning to acknowledge and accept mistakes as part of the learning process is essential for overcoming the grip of regret and moving forward in trading.

5. Revenge:

Revenge trading is perhaps the most destructive manifestation of emotions in trading. It occurs when traders seek to recoup losses by taking impulsive and reckless actions, driven by a desire for vengeance against the market. Revenge traders may abandon their trading plans, chase after losses, or increase position sizes in a desperate bid to "get back" at the market. However, revenge trading only serves to compound losses, as emotional decisions lead to further drawdowns and diminished capital. Breaking free from the cycle of revenge requires discipline, self-awareness, and a commitment to rational decision-making.

Emotions are an inherent part of human nature, and their influence extends into every aspect of trading. Fear, greed, hope, regret, and revenge are just a few of the emotions that traders grapple with on a daily basis, often with profound implications for their trading outcomes. By cultivating emotional awareness, practicing mindfulness, and adhering to disciplined trading strategies, traders can harness the power of emotions and use them as tools for informed decision-making, rather than allowing them to dictate their actions and undermine their success in the markets.

Unraveling the Mind's Maze: Cognitive Biases and Their Impact on Trading Decisions

In the world of financial markets, traders rely on their analytical skills and decision-making abilities to navigate complex trading landscapes. However, beneath the surface of rational analysis lies a myriad of cognitive biases that can distort perceptions, skew judgments, and lead to suboptimal trading decisions. Understanding these cognitive biases and their impact on trading is essential for traders seeking to improve their performance and achieve long-term success in the markets.

1. Confirmation Bias:

Confirmation bias is the tendency to seek out information that confirms pre-existing beliefs or hypotheses while ignoring or discounting evidence that contradicts them. In trading, confirmation bias can lead traders to selectively interpret information in a way that aligns with their existing views, reinforcing biases and preventing them from objectively assessing market conditions. For example, a trader may disregard signals indicating a potential reversal in a trend if it contradicts their bullish or bearish bias, leading to missed opportunities or losses.

2. Overconfidence Bias:

Overconfidence bias occurs when traders overestimate their abilities, knowledge, or predictive accuracy, leading them to take excessive risks or neglect proper risk management practices. Overconfident traders may believe they have an edge in the markets or that they can accurately predict future price movements with a high degree of certainty, leading to impulsive trading decisions and inflated expectations of returns. However, overconfidence can blind traders to the inherent uncertainty of the markets and increase the likelihood of significant losses.

3. Loss Aversion Bias:

Loss aversion bias refers to the tendency for individuals to prefer avoiding losses over acquiring equivalent gains, leading them to take irrational risks or hold onto losing positions in the hope of avoiding realizing a loss. In trading, loss aversion can manifest in various ways, such as traders refusing to cut their losses on losing trades, hoping for a reversal, or engaging in revenge trading to recoup losses quickly. This bias can lead to poor risk management, emotional decision-making, and significant drawdowns in trading accounts.

4. Anchoring Bias:

Anchoring bias occurs when individuals rely too heavily on a single piece of information or reference point (the "anchor") when making decisions, even when it may be irrelevant or misleading. In trading, anchoring bias can lead traders to fixate on specific price levels, such as entry or exit points, without considering other relevant factors or adjusting their strategies in response to changing market conditions. This can result in missed opportunities, as traders fail to adapt to new information or developments in the market.

5. Recency Bias:

Recency bias is the tendency to give greater weight to recent events or experiences when making decisions, while overlooking historical data or longer-term trends. In trading, recency bias can lead traders to overreact to short-term market fluctuations or trends, without considering the broader context or historical patterns. This can result in knee-jerk reactions to market movements, chasing after momentum without proper analysis, or failing to anticipate reversals in trend based on longer-term factors.

6. Gambler's Fallacy:

The gambler's fallacy is the mistaken belief that past events, particularly random events like coin flips or roulette spins, influence future outcomes. In trading, this bias can lead traders to make decisions based on perceived patterns or streaks in market movements, assuming that a trend will continue or reverse simply because it has persisted for a certain period. However, financial markets are not governed by the same principles as games of chance, and past performance is not necessarily indicative of future results.

Cognitive biases are inherent features of human psychology and can exert a profound influence on trading decisions. By understanding these biases and their impact on decision-making, traders can learn to recognize and mitigate their effects, improving their ability to make rational, informed decisions in the markets. Through disciplined analysis, emotional awareness, and a commitment to objective evaluation, traders can navigate the complexities of financial markets more effectively and increase their chances of long-term success.

Chapter 2: Developing a Winning Mindset

Cultivating Patience and Discipline: Keys to Success in Trading

In the dynamic and often unpredictable world of trading, success is not solely determined by market analysis or trading strategies. Patience and discipline stand as the cornerstone traits that separate consistently profitable traders from the rest. Cultivating these qualities is essential for navigating the complexities of financial markets and achieving long-term success. Here we explore the importance of patience and discipline in trading and offer practical tips for developing these critical attributes.

The Importance of Patience:

Patience is the ability to remain calm and composed in the face of uncertainty, waiting for the right opportunities to present themselves rather than rushing into impulsive decisions. In trading, patience is essential for several reasons:

1. Waiting for High-Quality Setups:

Successful traders understand that not every market condition is conducive to profitable trading. They patiently wait for high-quality setups that align with their trading strategies and offer favorable risk-reward ratios.

2. Allowing Trades to Develop:

Patience is required to allow trades to develop and reach their full potential. Rather than exiting prematurely at the first sign of a minor setback, patient traders give their trades time to play out, allowing for greater profit potential.

3. Avoiding Overtrading:

Impatient traders are prone to overtrading, entering into trades impulsively and without proper analysis. This can lead to increased transaction costs, higher levels of stress, and ultimately, diminished returns. Patience helps traders avoid falling into this trap and maintain discipline in their trading approach.

Practical Tips for Cultivating Patience:

- Develop a Trading Plan:

Create a detailed trading plan that outlines your strategy, including entry and exit criteria, risk management rules, and overall goals. Refer to your plan regularly and resist the temptation to deviate from it based on emotions or short-term market movements.

- Practice Mindfulness:

Stay present and focused on the current moment rather than dwelling on past losses or future uncertainties. Mindfulness techniques, such as meditation or deep breathing exercises, can help calm the mind and reduce impulsivity in trading decisions.

- Set Realistic Expectations:

Understand that trading is not a get-rich-quick scheme and that consistent profitability takes time and effort. Set realistic expectations for your trading performance and be patient as you work towards your long-term goals.

The Importance of Discipline:

Discipline is the ability to adhere to your trading plan and rules consistently, even in the face of temptation or adversity. It involves controlling impulses, managing emotions, and making decisions based on logic and analysis rather than instinct or intuition. Discipline is crucial in trading for several reasons:

1. Following a Trading Plan:

A well-defined trading plan serves as a roadmap for success in trading. Discipline is required to follow this plan rigorously, executing trades according to predefined criteria and resisting the urge to deviate from it based on emotions or market noise.

2. Implementing Risk Management:

Discipline is essential for implementing proper risk management techniques, such as setting stop-loss orders and position sizing. Traders who lack discipline may neglect these risk management principles, exposing themselves to unnecessary losses and jeopardizing their capital.

3. Overcoming Emotional Biases:

Emotional biases, such as fear, greed, and overconfidence, can cloud judgment and lead to irrational decision-making. Discipline helps traders overcome these biases by staying objective and sticking to their trading plan, even when emotions are running high.

Practical Tips for Cultivating Discipline:

- Establish Trading Rules:

Define clear and specific rules for your trading approach, including entry and exit criteria, risk management guidelines, and criteria for evaluating trade setups. Stick to these rules consistently, regardless of market conditions or emotional impulses.

- Keep a Trading Journal:

Maintain a detailed trading journal to track your trades, including entry and exit points, reasons for the trade, and outcomes. Reviewing your journal regularly can help identify patterns of behavior, strengths, and weaknesses, allowing you to make adjustments and improve your discipline over time.

- Practice Self-Control:

Develop self-awareness and self-control by learning to recognize and manage your emotions effectively. When faced with temptation or emotional triggers, take a step back, assess the situation objectively, and make decisions based on logic and analysis rather than impulse.

Patience and discipline are indispensable qualities for success in trading. By cultivating these attributes and incorporating them into your trading mindset and approach, you can navigate the challenges of financial markets more effectively, increase your consistency, and ultimately achieve your trading goals. Remember that developing patience and discipline is an ongoing process that requires dedication, self-awareness, and commitment, but the rewards in terms of improved trading performance and profitability are well worth the effort.

Building Confidence in Your Trading Abilities: A Roadmap to Success

Confidence is a powerful attribute that can greatly influence trading success. It's the belief in your own abilities, decisions, and strategies, even in the face of uncertainty and adversity. While confidence doesn't guarantee profitability, it's a critical component of a trader's mindset that can lead to better decision-making, increased resilience, and improved overall performance in the markets. Here we explore strategies for building and maintaining confidence in your trading abilities.

Acknowledge Your Strengths and Weaknesses:

Confidence begins with self-awareness. Take the time to assess your strengths and weaknesses as a trader. What are your areas of expertise? Where do you excel? Conversely, what are your weaknesses or areas for improvement? Understanding your strengths can boost confidence, while acknowledging weaknesses provides opportunities for growth and development.

Develop a Trading Plan and Stick to It:

A well-defined trading plan serves as a blueprint for success in trading. It outlines your trading strategy, including entry and exit criteria, risk management rules, and overall goals. Having a solid plan in place instills confidence by providing clarity and structure to your trading approach. However, it's not enough to simply have a plan; you must also have the discipline to stick to it consistently, even when faced with temptation or emotional impulses.

Practice Continuously and Learn from Experience:

Confidence grows through practice and experience. Take every opportunity to hone your trading skills, whether through simulated trading exercises, backtesting strategies, or live trading in the markets. Embrace both wins and losses as learning opportunities, and use each experience to refine your approach and build confidence in your abilities. Remember that trading is a journey of continuous improvement, and every trade provides valuable lessons that contribute to your growth as a trader.

Set Realistic Goals and Celebrate Milestones:

Setting realistic, achievable goals is essential for building confidence in your trading abilities. Break down your long-term objectives into smaller, manageable milestones, and celebrate each accomplishment along the way. Whether it's achieving a certain level of profitability, mastering a new trading strategy, or overcoming a particular challenge, acknowledging your progress reinforces confidence and motivates you to continue striving for success.

Surround Yourself with Supportive Communities:

Trading can be a solitary endeavor, but it doesn't have to be. Surround yourself with supportive communities of like-minded traders who share your passion for the markets. Engage in discussions, seek advice and feedback, and learn from the experiences of others. Being part of a supportive community not only provides valuable insights and encouragement but also fosters a sense of camaraderie and belonging that bolsters confidence during both the highs and lows of trading.

Manage Emotions and Stay Mentally Resilient:

Emotional resilience is crucial for maintaining confidence in trading. Learn to recognize and manage emotions such as fear, greed, and self-doubt that can undermine confidence and lead to irrational decision-making. Practice mindfulness techniques, such as deep breathing or visualization, to stay calm and focused during periods of market volatility or uncertainty. Cultivate a positive mindset and adopt a "growth mindset" approach, viewing setbacks as opportunities for learning and growth rather than failures.

MASTERING THE MARKETS: A COMPREHENSIVE GUIDE TO TRADING PSYCHOLOGY AND STRATEGIES

Building confidence in your trading abilities is a journey that requires self-awareness, discipline, practice, and support. By developing a solid trading plan, continuously improving your skills, setting realistic goals, surrounding yourself with supportive communities, and managing your emotions effectively, you can cultivate the confidence needed to navigate the challenges of trading successfully and achieve your financial goals. Remember that confidence is not an innate trait but rather a skill that can be developed and strengthened over time with dedication and perseverance.

Embracing Failure as a Learning Opportunity: The Path to Growth in Trading

In the high-stakes world of trading, failure is often viewed as a setback, a source of frustration, or even a sign of incompetence. However, seasoned traders understand that failure is an inevitable part of the journey towards success. Instead of fearing failure, they embrace it as a valuable learning opportunity that can lead to growth, resilience, and ultimately, improved trading performance. In this section, we explore the importance of embracing failure in trading and how it can serve as a catalyst for long-term success.

Understanding Failure in Trading:

Failure in trading can take many forms, whether it's a series of losing trades, a blown account, or a missed opportunity. Regardless of the specific circumstances, failure is often accompanied by feelings of disappointment, self-doubt, and frustration. However, rather than viewing failure as a final verdict on one's abilities or prospects as a trader, it's essential to recognize it as a natural and inevitable part of the learning process.

Learning from Failure:

Failure provides invaluable insights and lessons that can't be gained from success alone. When a trade goes wrong or a strategy fails to deliver the expected results, it's an opportunity to analyze what went wrong, identify areas for improvement, and adjust your approach accordingly. By reflecting on past failures and learning from mistakes, traders can refine their strategies, enhance their decision-making process, and ultimately become more resilient and adaptable in the face of future challenges.

Building Resilience and Mental Toughness:

Embracing failure is essential for building resilience and mental toughness in trading. Resilience is the ability to bounce back from setbacks, adapt to changing circumstances, and persevere in the pursuit of long-term goals. Failure tests resilience by challenging traders to overcome adversity, stay focused on their objectives, and maintain confidence in their abilities despite setbacks. Through repeated exposure to failure and the resilience it fosters, traders become better equipped to handle the inevitable ups and downs of trading with composure and grace.

Cultivating a Growth Mindset:

A growth mindset is characterized by a belief in the ability to learn, grow, and improve through effort and perseverance. Traders with a growth mindset view failure not as a reflection of their innate abilities or worth but as a temporary setback on the path to mastery. They approach failure with curiosity, seeking to understand the root causes of their mistakes and using them as opportunities for growth and development. By cultivating a growth mindset, traders become more resilient, adaptable, and open to new ideas and experiences, which ultimately leads to greater success in trading.

Practical Tips for Embracing Failure:

1. Keep a Trading Journal:

Maintain a detailed trading journal to document your trades, including entry and exit points, reasons for the trade, and outcomes. Reviewing your journal regularly can help identify patterns of behavior, strengths, and weaknesses, allowing you to learn from past mistakes and make improvements.

2. Seek Feedback and Support:

Surround yourself with supportive communities of traders who can offer feedback, advice, and encouragement. Sharing your experiences with others can provide valuable insights and perspective, helping you gain a deeper understanding of your trading performance and areas for improvement.

3. Stay Positive and Resilient:

Cultivate a positive mindset and focus on the progress you've made rather than dwelling on past failures. Develop coping strategies, such as mindfulness techniques or visualization exercises, to help you stay calm and focused during periods of adversity.

4. View Failure as Feedback:

Instead of viewing failure as a reflection of your abilities or worth, see it as valuable feedback that can help you grow and improve as a trader. Approach failure with a curious and open mindset, seeking to understand the lessons it has to offer and using them to become a better trader in the future.

Embracing failure as a learning opportunity is essential for growth and success in trading. By learning from past mistakes, building resilience, cultivating a growth mindset, and adopting practical strategies for embracing failure, traders can turn setbacks into stepping stones on the path to long-term profitability and fulfillment in trading. Remember that failure is not a final verdict but rather a temporary setback on the journey towards mastery, and by embracing it with humility and determination, you can unlock your full potential as a trader.

Setting Realistic Goals and Expectations: A Blueprint for Trading Success

In the fast-paced and often unpredictable world of trading, setting realistic goals and expectations is essential for long-term success and sustainability. While the allure of quick riches and overnight success may be tempting, seasoned traders understand that achieving consistent profitability requires patience, discipline, and a clear understanding of one's capabilities and limitations. In this section, we delve into the importance of setting realistic goals and expectations in trading and offer practical tips for doing so effectively.

The Importance of Setting Realistic Goals:

Setting realistic goals provides traders with a roadmap for success, guiding their actions and decisions in the markets. Realistic goals are specific, measurable, achievable, relevant, and time-bound (SMART), providing clarity and focus to a trader's efforts. Whether it's achieving a certain level of profitability, mastering a new trading strategy, or building a consistent track record, setting realistic goals helps traders stay motivated, accountable, and on track towards their objectives.

Avoiding Unrealistic Expectations:

While ambition and aspiration are admirable traits, unrealistic expectations can set traders up for disappointment, frustration, and ultimately, failure. Unrealistic expectations often stem from a lack of understanding of the realities of trading, such as the inherent risks, uncertainties, and challenges involved. Whether it's expecting to double one's account in a month or never experiencing a losing trade, unrealistic expectations can lead to impulsive decision-making, excessive risk-taking, and emotional distress when reality inevitably falls short of expectations.

Practical Tips for Setting Realistic Goals and Expectations:
1. Start with Self-Assessment:

Begin by conducting an honest assessment of your trading experience, skills, strengths, and weaknesses. Identify your risk tolerance, financial resources, time commitment, and other factors that may influence your trading goals and expectations. Be realistic about what you can achieve given your current circumstances and limitations.

2. Set Clear and Achievable Goals:

Define clear and specific trading goals that are aligned with your abilities, resources, and objectives. Break down long-term goals into smaller, manageable milestones that are achievable within a realistic timeframe. For example, instead of aiming to double your account overnight, focus on achieving a consistent monthly return that aligns with your risk tolerance and trading strategy.

3. Be Flexible and Adaptive:

While it's important to set goals and expectations, it's equally important to remain flexible and adaptive in the face of changing market conditions and circumstances. Be prepared to adjust your goals and expectations as needed based on new information, feedback, and experiences. Remember that trading is a dynamic and evolving process, and flexibility is key to long-term success.

4. Focus on Process Over Outcome:

Instead of fixating solely on the end result or outcome of your trades, focus on the process and execution of your trading strategy. Emphasize factors within your control, such as proper risk management, disciplined execution, and continuous learning and improvement. By focusing on the process rather than the outcome, you can maintain a more balanced perspective and avoid becoming overly attached to short-term results.

5. Manage Emotions and Stay Patient:

Emotions play a significant role in shaping traders' goals and expectations, often leading to irrational decision-making and unrealistic beliefs about the markets. Learn to manage your emotions effectively, stay patient, and maintain a long-term perspective in your trading approach. Remember that success in trading is not measured by short-term gains or losses but by consistent profitability and sustainable growth over time.

Setting realistic goals and expectations is essential for success and sustainability in trading. By conducting a thorough self-assessment, setting clear and achievable goals, remaining flexible and adaptive, focusing on the process over the outcome, and managing emotions effectively, traders can increase their chances of achieving long-term profitability and fulfillment in trading. Remember that trading is a journey, not a destination, and by setting realistic goals and expectations, you can navigate the challenges of the markets with confidence and resilience.

Chapter 3: Overcoming Emotional Biases

Navigating the Emotional Minefield: Recognizing and Managing FOMO and FOLO in Trading

In the highly competitive world of trading, emotions play a significant role in shaping decision-making processes and trading outcomes. Among the myriad of emotions that traders experience, two common ones are Fear of Missing Out (FOMO) and Fear of Losing (FOLO). These emotions can lead to impulsive actions, irrational decision-making, and ultimately, detrimental effects on trading performance.

Understanding FOMO and FOLO:

1. Fear of Missing Out (FOMO):

FOMO is the apprehension or anxiety that one is missing out on profitable opportunities or gains in the market. It arises from the fear of not being able to capitalize on potential profits or trends and the desire to be part of the action. Traders experiencing FOMO may feel compelled to enter trades hastily, chase after momentum, or increase position sizes beyond their risk tolerance, driven by the fear of being left behind.

2. Fear of Losing (FOLO):

FOLO, on the other hand, is the aversion or dread of incurring losses or missing out on potential gains. It stems from the fear of making mistakes, losing capital, or experiencing failure in trading. Traders experiencing FOLO may become overly cautious or risk-averse, hesitating to enter trades or exiting winning positions prematurely to avoid losses, even if it means missing out on potential profits.

Impact of FOMO and FOLO on Trading:

Both FOMO and FOLO can have detrimental effects on trading performance, leading to suboptimal decision-making, increased stress, and diminished returns. Traders driven by FOMO may engage in impulsive trading, entering trades without proper analysis or risk management, and chasing after market trends that may have already peaked. Conversely, traders driven by FOLO may miss out on profitable opportunities, hesitate to pull the trigger on trades, or exit winning positions prematurely, leading to missed gains and underperformance relative to their potential.

Managing FOMO and FOLO Effectively:

1. Develop a Trading Plan:

Having a well-defined trading plan is essential for managing both FOMO and FOLO. A trading plan outlines your strategy, including entry and exit criteria, risk management rules, and overall goals. By adhering to your plan consistently, you can reduce the influence of emotions on your trading decisions and maintain discipline in the face of FOMO and FOLO.

2. Practice Patience and Discipline:

Patience and discipline are key virtues for managing FOMO and FOLO effectively. Practice patience by waiting for high-quality trade setups that align with your trading strategy and risk parameters. Exercise discipline by sticking to your trading plan and avoiding impulsive actions driven by emotions. Remember that successful trading is a marathon, not a sprint, and consistent profitability requires a long-term perspective.

3. Set Realistic Goals and Expectations:

Setting realistic goals and expectations helps mitigate the effects of both FOMO and FOLO. Define clear and achievable trading goals that align with your risk tolerance, financial resources, and trading style. Break down long-term goals into smaller, manageable milestones, and celebrate each accomplishment along the way. By setting realistic goals and expectations, you can reduce the pressure to perform and focus on long-term growth and development in trading.

4. Practice Mindfulness and Self-Awareness:

Mindfulness techniques, such as deep breathing, meditation, or visualization, can help manage emotions and increase self-awareness in trading. When you feel FOMO or FOLO creeping in, take a step back, acknowledge your emotions without judgment, and refocus your attention on the present moment. By practicing mindfulness, you can cultivate a more balanced perspective, reduce impulsive behavior, and make better-informed decisions in trading.

5. Learn from Experience:

Every trade provides an opportunity to learn and grow as a trader. Whether it's a winning trade or a losing trade, take the time to reflect on the outcome, analyze what went right or wrong, and identify areas for improvement. By learning from experience, you can gain valuable insights into your trading performance, refine your strategies, and become more resilient in the face of future challenges.

Recognizing and managing FOMO and FOLO is essential for success and sustainability in trading. By developing a clear trading plan, practicing patience and discipline, setting realistic goals and expectations, practicing mindfulness and self-awareness, and learning from experience, traders can mitigate the effects of these emotions and make more informed, rational decisions in the markets. Remember that trading is as much a psychological game as it is a technical one, and mastering your emotions is key to achieving long-term success and profitability.

Mastering the Mind: Strategies for Dealing with Overconfidence and Confirmation Bias in Trading

In trading, success depends not only on technical analysis and market knowledge but also on mastering the psychological aspects of decision-making. Two common cognitive biases that traders often grapple with are overconfidence and confirmation bias. These biases can lead to irrational decision-making, distorted perceptions of risk, and ultimately, detrimental effects on trading performance.

Understanding Overconfidence and Confirmation Bias:

1. Overconfidence:

Overconfidence is the tendency to overestimate one's abilities, knowledge, or predictive accuracy, leading to excessive risk-taking and unrealistic expectations of success. In trading, overconfident traders may believe they have an edge in the markets or that they can accurately predict future price movements with a high degree of certainty. This can lead to impulsive trading decisions, failure to adhere to risk management principles, and ultimately, significant losses.

2. Confirmation Bias:

Confirmation bias is the tendency to seek out information that confirms pre-existing beliefs or hypotheses while ignoring or discounting evidence that contradicts them. In trading, confirmation bias can lead traders to selectively interpret information in a way that aligns with their existing views, reinforcing biases and preventing them from objectively assessing market conditions. This can result in missed opportunities, poor risk management, and distorted perceptions of market trends.

Impact of Overconfidence and Confirmation Bias on Trading:

Both overconfidence and confirmation bias can have detrimental effects on trading performance, leading to suboptimal decision-making, increased risk exposure, and diminished returns. Overconfident traders may take excessive risks, neglect proper risk management practices, and fail to acknowledge the inherent uncertainty of the markets. Similarly, traders influenced by confirmation bias may disregard warning signs, overlook contradictory evidence, and persist in holding onto losing positions, leading to missed opportunities and significant losses.

Strategies for Dealing with Overconfidence and Confirmation Bias:

1. Maintain Humility:

Recognize that trading is inherently uncertain and that no one has all the answers. Adopt a humble mindset and acknowledge the limitations of your knowledge and abilities. Stay open to feedback, constructive criticism, and alternative viewpoints, and be willing to adjust your beliefs and assumptions based on new information.

2. Cultivate Self-Awareness:

Develop self-awareness by monitoring your thoughts, emotions, and behaviors in trading. Pay attention to instances of overconfidence or confirmation bias and examine the underlying reasons behind them. Keep a trading journal to document your trades, decisions, and emotions, and use it as a tool for reflection and self-improvement.

3. Challenge Your Assumptions:

Actively challenge your assumptions and beliefs in trading by seeking out contradictory evidence and alternative perspectives. Question the basis for your trading decisions, and be willing to entertain the possibility that you may be wrong. Engage in critical thinking and objective analysis, rather than relying solely on gut instincts or intuition.

4. Diversify Your Analysis:

Expand your sources of information and analysis beyond your preconceived notions and biases. Seek out diverse viewpoints, market data, and technical indicators to gain a more comprehensive understanding of market conditions. Avoid relying solely on information that confirms your existing beliefs and be open to considering alternative viewpoints.

5. Implement Risk Management:

Implement proper risk management techniques to mitigate the effects of overconfidence and confirmation bias on trading. Set clear risk parameters, such as stop-loss orders and position sizing limits, and adhere to them consistently. By limiting your risk exposure and preserving capital, you can reduce the potential impact of impulsive or biased trading decisions.

Dealing with overconfidence and confirmation bias is essential for success and sustainability in trading. By maintaining humility, cultivating self-awareness, challenging assumptions, diversifying analysis, and implementing risk management, traders can mitigate the effects of these biases and make more informed, rational decisions in the markets. Remember that mastering the psychological aspects of trading is an ongoing process that requires dedication, self-discipline, and a willingness to learn and adapt. By mastering your mind, you can unlock your full potential as a trader and increase your chances of long-term success and profitability.

Staying on Course: Strategies for Avoiding Revenge Trading and Chasing Losses in Trading

In trading, losses are an inevitable part of the game. However, how traders respond to those losses can make all the difference between long-term success and failure. Two common pitfalls that traders often fall into after experiencing losses are revenge trading and chasing losses. These behaviors can lead to impulsive decision-making, increased risk exposure, and ultimately, further losses.

Understanding Revenge Trading and Chasing Losses:

1. Revenge Trading:

Revenge trading occurs when traders seek to recoup losses quickly by taking impulsive and reckless actions in the market. It is driven by emotions such as frustration, anger, and a desire for vengeance against the market. Revenge traders may abandon their trading plan, increase position sizes beyond prudent levels, or take speculative trades in a desperate bid to "get back" at the market. However, revenge trading only serves to compound losses, as emotional decisions lead to further drawdowns and diminished capital.

2. Chasing Losses:

Chasing losses is the tendency to increase risk exposure or deviate from one's trading plan in an attempt to recover losses incurred in trading. It arises from the fear of realizing losses and the desire to break even or turn a losing trade into a winner. Chasing losses can lead traders to take impulsive actions, such as doubling down on losing positions, moving stop-loss orders further away, or entering new trades without proper analysis or risk management. However, chasing losses often leads to further losses, as traders become increasingly exposed to market volatility and unpredictable price movements.

Impact of Revenge Trading and Chasing Losses on Trading:

Both revenge trading and chasing losses can have detrimental effects on trading performance, leading to a cycle of emotional decision-making, increased risk exposure, and diminished returns. Traders who engage in revenge trading or chasing losses often experience heightened levels of stress, anxiety, and frustration, which can cloud judgment and impair rational decision-making. This can result in further losses, deeper drawdowns, and significant setbacks to long-term profitability and sustainability in trading.

Strategies for Avoiding Revenge Trading and Chasing Losses:

1. Maintain Emotional Control:

Emotional control is essential for avoiding revenge trading and chasing losses in trading. Learn to recognize and manage emotions such as frustration, anger, and fear, which can lead to impulsive decision-making. Practice mindfulness techniques, such as deep breathing or visualization, to stay calm and focused during periods of market volatility or uncertainty. Remember that emotional decisions are rarely rational or beneficial in trading, and maintaining emotional control is key to long-term success.

2. Stick to Your Trading Plan:

Having a well-defined trading plan is crucial for avoiding revenge trading and chasing losses. A trading plan outlines your strategy, including entry and exit criteria, risk management rules, and overall goals. By adhering to your plan consistently, you can reduce the influence of emotions on your trading decisions and maintain discipline in the face of adversity. Trust in your plan and avoid deviating from it based on impulsive emotions or short-term market movements.

3. Accept and Manage Losses:

Losses are an inevitable part of trading and should be viewed as learning opportunities rather than failures. Accept that losses are a natural and unavoidable aspect of the trading process and focus on managing them effectively. Set clear risk parameters, such as stop-loss orders and position sizing limits, and adhere to them rigorously. By limiting your risk exposure and preserving capital, you can mitigate the impact of losses on your trading account and avoid the temptation to engage in revenge trading or chasing losses.

4. Take a Break if Necessary:

If you find yourself feeling overwhelmed or emotionally compromised after experiencing losses, it may be beneficial to take a break from trading temporarily. Stepping away from the markets allows you to regain perspective, recharge emotionally, and refocus your energies on self-care and personal well-being. Use this time to reflect on your trading performance, identify areas for improvement, and develop strategies for managing risk and emotions more effectively in the future.

5. Seek Support and Accountability:

Surround yourself with supportive communities of traders who can offer guidance, feedback, and encouragement during challenging times. Share your experiences with others, seek advice from mentors or experienced traders, and hold yourself accountable for your actions and decisions. Having a support network can provide valuable insights and perspective, help you stay disciplined and focused on your long-term goals, and reduce the temptation to engage in revenge trading or chasing losses.

Avoiding revenge trading and chasing losses is essential for success and sustainability in trading. By maintaining emotional control, sticking to your trading plan, accepting and managing losses, taking breaks when necessary, and seeking support and accountability, traders can mitigate the effects of these destructive behaviors and make more informed, rational decisions in the markets. Remember that trading is a marathon, not a sprint, and maintaining discipline and patience is key to achieving long-term success and profitability.

Mastering Self-Control: Strategies for Controlling Impulsive Behavior and Overtrading in Trading

Two common pitfalls that traders often struggle with are impulsive behavior and overtrading. These behaviors can lead to reckless decision-making, increased risk exposure, and ultimately, detrimental effects on trading performance.

Understanding Impulsive Behavior and Overtrading:

1. Impulsive Behavior:

Impulsive behavior refers to actions that are made hastily, without careful consideration of their consequences. In trading, impulsive traders may enter or exit trades impulsively, without proper analysis or adherence to their trading plan. Impulsive behavior is often driven by emotions such as greed, fear of missing out (FOMO), or a desire for instant gratification. However, impulsive decisions in trading can lead to increased risk exposure, diminished returns, and significant losses.

2. Overtrading:

Overtrading occurs when traders execute an excessive number of trades within a short period, often in response to emotional triggers or market noise. Overtrading is fueled by the desire to be constantly involved in the markets and the misconception that more trades equate to greater profits. However, overtrading leads to higher transaction costs, increased stress, and diminished focus on high-quality trade setups. It can also result in fatigue, burnout, and emotional exhaustion, further exacerbating impulsive behavior.

Impact of Impulsive Behavior and Overtrading on Trading:

Both impulsive behavior and overtrading can have detrimental effects on trading performance, leading to suboptimal decision-making, increased risk exposure, and diminished returns. Impulsive traders are more likely to deviate from their trading plan, abandon proper risk management practices, and make decisions based on emotions rather than logic or analysis. Similarly, overtrading leads to excessive transaction costs, increased stress, and diminished focus on high-quality trade setups, ultimately resulting in diminished profitability and sustainability in trading.

Strategies for Controlling Impulsive Behavior and Overtrading:

1. Develop a Trading Plan and Stick to It:

Having a well-defined trading plan is essential for controlling impulsive behavior and overtrading. A trading plan outlines your strategy, including entry and exit criteria, risk management rules, and overall goals. By adhering to your plan consistently, you can reduce the influence of emotions on your trading decisions and maintain discipline in the face of market volatility or uncertainty.

2. Practice Patience and Discipline:

Patience and discipline are key virtues for controlling impulsive behavior and overtrading in trading. Practice patience by waiting for high-quality trade setups that align with your trading strategy and risk parameters. Exercise discipline by sticking to your trading plan and avoiding impulsive actions driven by emotions or short-term market movements.

3. Set Clear Risk Parameters:

Establish clear risk parameters, such as stop-loss orders, position sizing limits, and maximum daily loss limits, and adhere to them rigorously. By setting clear risk parameters, you can limit your risk exposure and prevent impulsive behavior and overtrading from leading to excessive losses or drawdowns.

4. Monitor Your Emotions:

Develop self-awareness by monitoring your thoughts, emotions, and behaviors in trading. Pay attention to instances of impulsive behavior or overtrading and examine the underlying reasons behind them. Use mindfulness techniques, such as deep breathing or visualization, to stay calm and focused during periods of market volatility or uncertainty.

5. Take Regular Breaks:

Take regular breaks from trading to rest and recharge both mentally and physically. Stepping away from the markets allows you to regain perspective, reduce stress, and refocus your energies on self-care and personal well-being. Use this time to reflect on your trading performance, identify patterns of behavior, and develop strategies for controlling impulsive behavior and overtrading more effectively.

Controlling impulsive behavior and overtrading is essential for success and sustainability in trading. By developing a clear trading plan, practicing patience and discipline, setting clear risk parameters, monitoring your emotions, and taking regular breaks from trading, traders can mitigate the effects of impulsive behavior and overtrading and make more informed, rational decisions in the markets. Remember that mastering the psychological aspects of trading is an ongoing process that requires dedication, self-discipline, and a commitment to continuous improvement. By mastering self-control, you can unlock your full potential as a trader and increase your chances of long-term success and profitability.

Chapter 4: Building Effective Risk Management Strategies

Navigating the Markets: Understanding the Importance of Risk Management in Trading

In the dynamic and often unpredictable world of trading, success is not solely determined by picking winning trades but also by effectively managing risk. Risk management is a fundamental aspect of trading that involves identifying, assessing, and mitigating potential risks to protect capital and maximize returns.

The Importance of Risk Management:

1. Preservation of Capital:

One of the primary objectives of risk management is the preservation of capital. By controlling risk exposure and limiting the potential downside of trades, traders can protect their trading capital from significant losses. Preservation of capital is essential for long-term sustainability in trading, as it ensures that traders have the financial resources to continue trading and take advantage of profitable opportunities in the future.

2. Consistent Returns:

Effective risk management contributes to the generation of consistent returns over time. By adhering to sound risk management principles, traders can minimize the impact of losses on their overall performance and maintain a steady trajectory of profitability. Consistent returns are essential for building confidence, attracting investors, and achieving long-term financial goals in trading.

3. Psychological Well-being:

Risk management also plays a crucial role in maintaining psychological well-being and emotional stability in trading. By implementing risk management techniques, traders can reduce the emotional impact of losses and avoid succumbing to fear, greed, or impulsivity. This helps traders stay disciplined, focused, and resilient in the face of adversity, leading to better decision-making and improved trading performance.

Key Principles of Risk Management:

1. Define Risk Tolerance:

Before engaging in trading, it's essential to define your risk tolerance and establish clear risk parameters. Risk tolerance refers to the level of risk that you are comfortable taking on each trade or portfolio. Assess your financial situation, investment goals, and psychological disposition to determine an appropriate level of risk tolerance that aligns with your trading style and objectives.

2. Set Stop-Loss Orders:

Implementing stop-loss orders is a fundamental risk management technique that helps limit losses and protect capital. A stop-loss order is an instruction to close a position automatically when the price reaches a predetermined level. By setting stop-loss orders at strategic levels based on technical analysis or risk-reward considerations, traders can minimize the impact of adverse price movements and exit losing trades before they escalate into significant losses.

3. Diversify Your Portfolio:

Diversification is another essential principle of risk management that involves spreading risk across different assets, markets, or trading strategies. By diversifying your portfolio, you can reduce the concentration risk associated with individual trades or market sectors and increase the resilience of your overall portfolio to adverse market conditions. Diversification helps mitigate the impact of unexpected events or market fluctuations on your trading performance and enhances the consistency of returns over time.

4. Manage Position Sizes:

Proper position sizing is critical for effective risk management in trading. Determine the appropriate position size for each trade based on your risk tolerance, account size, and the potential impact on your overall portfolio. Avoid risking more than a small percentage of your trading capital on any single trade to minimize the risk of significant losses and ensure that you can withstand temporary drawdowns without jeopardizing your long-term financial goals.

Practical Strategies for Implementing Risk Management:

1. Develop a Trading Plan:

Create a comprehensive trading plan that includes clear entry and exit criteria, risk management rules, and overall goals. Stick to your trading plan consistently and avoid deviating from it based on emotions or short-term market fluctuations.

2. Monitor Your Risk Exposure:

Regularly monitor your risk exposure and assess the potential impact of trades on your overall portfolio. Adjust your position sizes, stop-loss levels, and trading strategies as needed to maintain an optimal risk-reward balance and protect capital.

3. Review and Learn from Mistakes:

Review your trading performance regularly and analyze the outcomes of your trades. Identify areas for improvement, learn from mistakes, and refine your risk management techniques accordingly. Continuous learning and adaptation are key to mastering risk management in trading and achieving long-term success.

Understanding the importance of risk management is essential for success and sustainability in trading. By preserving capital, generating consistent returns, and maintaining psychological well-being, effective risk management helps traders navigate the challenges of the markets and achieve their financial goals. By adhering to key principles such as defining risk tolerance, setting stop-loss orders, diversifying portfolios, and managing position sizes, traders can implement practical strategies for managing risk effectively and increasing their chances of long-term success in trading.

Mastering Trade Management: Setting Proper Stop-Loss and Take-Profit Levels

Setting proper stop-loss and take-profit levels is essential for managing risk, preserving capital, and maximizing returns. Stop-loss and take-profit orders are fundamental tools that help traders control risk exposure, protect profits, and maintain discipline in their trading approach.

The Importance of Stop-Loss and Take-Profit Levels:

1. Risk Management:

Setting proper stop-loss levels is crucial for managing risk in trading. A stop-loss order is an instruction to close a position automatically when the price reaches a predetermined level, limiting potential losses on a trade. By defining clear stop-loss levels based on technical analysis, risk-reward considerations, or volatility metrics, traders can protect their capital from significant drawdowns and preserve their trading account for future opportunities.

2. Profit Protection:

Take-profit levels are equally important for protecting profits and capitalizing on favorable price movements. A take-profit order is an instruction to close a position automatically when the price reaches a predetermined profit target, locking in gains and realizing profits on a trade. By setting proper take-profit levels based on technical analysis, support and resistance levels, or profit targets, traders can secure profits and avoid the pitfalls of greed and overtrading.

Key Considerations for Setting Stop-Loss and Take-Profit Levels:

1. Technical Analysis:

Utilize technical analysis techniques, such as chart patterns, trendlines, and indicators, to identify key levels of support and resistance. These levels can serve as potential stop-loss and take-profit levels, providing reference points for managing risk and targeting profits. Consider factors such as historical price action, trend strength, and market volatility when setting stop-loss and take-profit levels based on technical analysis.

2. Risk-Reward Ratio:

Maintain a favorable risk-reward ratio when setting stop-loss and take-profit levels for each trade. A risk-reward ratio compares the potential reward of a trade to the potential risk, helping traders assess the viability of a trade and manage risk effectively. Aim for a risk-reward ratio of at least 1:2 or higher, ensuring that potential profits outweigh potential losses and providing a cushion against adverse market movements.

3. Volatility and Market Conditions:

Consider market volatility and prevailing market conditions when setting stop-loss and take-profit levels. Higher volatility may require wider stop-loss and take-profit levels to account for larger price swings and fluctuations. Conversely, lower volatility may allow for tighter stop-loss and take-profit levels to maximize profit potential and minimize risk exposure. Adapt your stop-loss and take-profit levels accordingly based on changing market conditions and volatility.

Practical Strategies for Setting Stop-Loss and Take-Profit Levels:

1. Plan Your Trades:

Before entering a trade, establish clear stop-loss and take-profit levels as part of your trading plan. Define your risk tolerance, profit targets, and exit criteria based on thorough analysis and objective assessment of market conditions. Stick to your trading plan consistently and avoid making impulsive decisions based on emotions or short-term market fluctuations.

2. Use Trailing Stops:

Consider using trailing stop-loss orders to lock in profits and protect against adverse price movements. A trailing stop-loss order adjusts dynamically with the price movement, moving in the direction of the trade and locking in gains as the price moves in favor of the trade. Trailing stops allow traders to capture profits while giving the trade room to breathe and potentially ride out trends for extended gains.

3. Monitor Trade Progress:

Regularly monitor the progress of your trades and adjust stop-loss and take-profit levels as needed based on evolving market conditions. Consider trailing stop-loss orders, adjusting stop-loss levels to breakeven once a certain profit threshold is reached, or scaling out of positions gradually to secure profits while allowing for further upside potential.

4. Review and Learn from Trades:

Review your trading performance regularly and analyze the outcomes of your trades. Identify patterns of success or failure, learn from mistakes, and refine your approach to setting stop-loss and take-profit levels accordingly. Continuous learning and adaptation are key to mastering trade management and optimizing risk-reward ratios in trading.

Setting proper stop-loss and take-profit levels is essential for effective trade management and risk control in trading. By defining clear stop-loss and take-profit levels based on technical analysis, risk-reward considerations, and market conditions, traders can protect their capital, maximize profits, and maintain discipline in their trading approach. By adhering to key considerations and practical strategies for setting stop-loss and take-profit levels, traders can increase their chances of long-term success and profitability in trading.

Mastering Position Sizing: Strategies for Effective Risk Management in Trading

Position sizing is a critical component of risk management in trading, allowing traders to control risk exposure, preserve capital, and optimize returns. Proper position sizing techniques help traders manage the inherent uncertainties of the market and ensure that each trade aligns with their risk tolerance and overall trading strategy.

The Importance of Position Sizing:

1. Risk Management:

Position sizing is essential for managing risk in trading. By determining the appropriate size of each position based on risk parameters such as stop-loss levels, account size, and risk tolerance, traders can limit the potential downside of trades and protect their capital from significant losses. Effective risk management through position sizing is critical for long-term sustainability and profitability in trading.

2. Consistent Returns:

Proper position sizing contributes to the generation of consistent returns over time. By aligning position sizes with risk-reward considerations and overall portfolio objectives, traders can maintain a steady trajectory of profitability and avoid excessive drawdowns that can erode trading capital. Consistent returns are essential for building confidence, attracting investors, and achieving long-term financial goals in trading.

Key Position Sizing Techniques:

1. Fixed Percentage Risk:

The fixed percentage risk method involves allocating a fixed percentage of trading capital to each trade based on risk tolerance. For example, a trader may decide to risk 1% of their account capital on each trade. The position size is calculated based on the distance between the entry price and the stop-loss level, ensuring that the total risk per trade remains consistent regardless of market conditions or account size.

2. Volatility-Based Position Sizing:

Volatility-based position sizing adjusts position sizes dynamically based on market volatility. Traders may use indicators such as average true range (ATR) to measure volatility and adjust position sizes accordingly. In highly volatile markets, position sizes may be reduced to account for larger price swings and increased risk, while in low-volatility markets, position sizes may be increased to capitalize on smaller price movements.

3. Fixed Dollar Amount:

The fixed dollar amount method involves risking a fixed dollar amount on each trade, regardless of account size or risk tolerance. For example, a trader may decide to risk $100 on each trade. The position size is calculated based on the distance between the entry price and the stop-loss level, ensuring that the total dollar risk per trade remains consistent.

Practical Strategies for Implementing Position Sizing Techniques:

1. Determine Risk Tolerance:

Before implementing position sizing techniques, assess your risk tolerance and establish clear risk parameters for each trade. Consider factors such as account size, trading goals, and psychological disposition to determine an appropriate level of risk tolerance that aligns with your overall trading strategy.

2. Calculate Position Size:

Use position sizing formulas or calculators to determine the appropriate position size for each trade based on your chosen position sizing technique and risk parameters. Consider factors such as entry price, stop-loss level, account size, and risk percentage to calculate position sizes accurately.

3. Review and Adjust:

Regularly review your position sizing techniques and adjust them as needed based on changing market conditions, account size, or risk tolerance. Monitor the performance of your trades, identify areas for improvement, and refine your position sizing techniques accordingly to optimize risk management and maximize returns over time.

4. Practice Consistency:

Maintain consistency in your position sizing techniques and adhere to your risk parameters consistently across all trades. Avoid making impulsive decisions or deviating from your position sizing strategy based on emotions or short-term market fluctuations. Consistency is key to effective risk management and long-term success in trading.

Implementing position sizing techniques is essential for effective risk management and profitability in trading. By aligning position sizes with risk parameters such as stop-loss levels, account size, and risk tolerance, traders can control risk exposure, preserve capital, and optimize returns. By understanding the importance of position sizing, mastering key position sizing techniques, and implementing practical strategies for effective position sizing, traders can increase their chances of long-term success and sustainability in trading.

Balancing Risk and Reward: The Importance of Diversifying Your Trading Portfolio

Diversification is often hailed as a fundamental principle for managing risk and maximizing returns. Diversifying your trading portfolio involves spreading your investments across a variety of assets, markets, or trading strategies to reduce concentration risk and increase the resilience of your overall portfolio to adverse market conditions.

The Importance of Diversification:

1. Risk Mitigation:

Diversification is essential for managing risk in trading. By spreading your investments across different assets or markets, you can reduce the impact of individual events or market fluctuations on your overall portfolio. Diversification helps minimize the risk of significant losses from any single trade or market sector and ensures that your portfolio is less susceptible to adverse market conditions or unexpected events.

2. Preservation of Capital:

Diversification helps preserve capital by minimizing the potential impact of losses on your overall portfolio. Even if one asset or market experiences a downturn, gains in other areas of your portfolio can offset losses and help maintain the value of your investment. Preservation of capital is essential for long-term sustainability in trading, as it ensures that you have the financial resources to continue trading and take advantage of profitable opportunities in the future.

3. Smoother Returns:

Diversification can lead to smoother and more consistent returns over time. By spreading your investments across different assets or markets with uncorrelated price movements, you can reduce the volatility of your overall portfolio and achieve a more stable performance. Smoother returns help build confidence, reduce emotional stress, and enhance the predictability of outcomes, contributing to a more sustainable and rewarding trading experience.

Key Benefits of Diversifying Your Trading Portfolio:

1. Reduced Concentration Risk:

Diversification helps reduce concentration risk by spreading investments across multiple assets, markets, or trading strategies. Concentration risk arises when a significant portion of your portfolio is allocated to a single asset class or market sector, increasing the vulnerability of your portfolio to adverse events or market fluctuations. Diversification ensures that your portfolio is well-balanced and less reliant on the performance of any individual asset or market.

2. Increased Resilience:

Diversification increases the resilience of your portfolio to unexpected events or market shocks. By investing in assets with low or negative correlations, you can offset losses in one area of your portfolio with gains in another, helping cushion the impact of adverse market conditions. A diversified portfolio is better equipped to weather volatility, uncertainty, and economic downturns, providing stability and protection against downside risk.

3. Enhanced Opportunities for Growth:

Diversification opens up opportunities for growth by exposing your portfolio to a wider range of investment opportunities. By investing in different asset classes, markets, or trading strategies, you can capitalize on diverse sources of potential returns and take advantage of profitable opportunities across various sectors or industries. Diversification allows you to optimize risk-reward ratios and maximize the growth potential of your portfolio over time.

Practical Strategies for Diversifying Your Trading Portfolio:

1. Spread Investments Across Asset Classes:

Diversify your portfolio by investing in different asset classes, such as equities, bonds, commodities, currencies, or cryptocurrencies. Each asset class has unique risk-return characteristics and behaves differently under varying market conditions, providing diversification benefits and enhancing the resilience of your portfolio.

2. Allocate Across Markets and Geographies:

Diversify your portfolio by investing in different markets and geographical regions. Spread your investments across domestic and international markets, developed and emerging economies, and regions with diverse economic drivers and growth prospects. Geographic diversification helps reduce country-specific risks and exposure to localized events or geopolitical uncertainties.

3. Utilize Multiple Trading Strategies:

Diversify your portfolio by employing multiple trading strategies with different risk-return profiles. For example, combine trend-following, mean-reversion, and breakout strategies to capture opportunities across different market environments. Each trading strategy has strengths and weaknesses, and diversifying across strategies helps mitigate the impact of strategy-specific risks and enhances the consistency of returns.

4. Monitor and Rebalance Regularly:

Regularly monitor the performance of your portfolio and rebalance as needed to maintain your desired level of diversification. Review your asset allocation, risk exposure, and performance metrics regularly, and adjust your portfolio allocation accordingly based on changing market conditions, investment goals, and risk tolerance. Rebalancing ensures that your portfolio remains aligned with your objectives and optimizes risk-return characteristics over time.

Diversifying your trading portfolio is essential for managing risk, preserving capital, and maximizing returns in trading. By spreading your investments across different assets, markets, and trading strategies, you can reduce concentration risk, increase resilience, and enhance opportunities for growth. By understanding the importance of diversification and implementing practical strategies for diversifying your trading portfolio effectively, you can optimize risk-reward ratios and increase your chances of long-term success and profitability in trading.

Chapter 5: Enhancing Decision-Making Skills

Striking the Balance: Utilizing Technical and Fundamental Analysis Wisely in Trading

Two primary methodologies reign supreme: technical analysis and fundamental analysis. While each approach offers unique insights into market dynamics, successful traders often employ a combination of both to make informed decisions.

Understanding Technical and Fundamental Analysis:

1. Technical Analysis:

Technical analysis involves analyzing historical price data, volume, and other market indicators to forecast future price movements. Traders who use technical analysis rely on charts, patterns, and technical indicators to identify trends, support and resistance levels, and entry and exit points for trades. Technical analysis is based on the premise that historical price patterns tend to repeat themselves and can provide valuable insights into market sentiment and potential price direction.

2. Fundamental Analysis:

Fundamental analysis involves evaluating the underlying factors that drive the value of an asset, such as economic indicators, company financials, industry trends, and geopolitical events. Traders who use fundamental analysis assess factors such as earnings growth, revenue projections, interest rates, and macroeconomic trends to determine the intrinsic value of an asset and its potential for future growth or decline. Fundamental analysis seeks to identify mispriced assets and capitalize on discrepancies between intrinsic value and market price.

The Importance of Integrating Technical and Fundamental Analysis:

1. Comprehensive Market Analysis:

Integrating technical and fundamental analysis allows traders to gain a comprehensive understanding of market dynamics and make more informed trading decisions. While technical analysis provides insights into short-term price movements and market sentiment, fundamental analysis offers insights into long-term trends, economic fundamentals, and underlying market conditions. By combining both approaches, traders can obtain a more holistic view of the market and identify high-probability trading opportunities.

2. Confirmation and Validation:

Technical and fundamental analysis can complement each other by providing confirmation and validation of trading signals. For example, a technical breakout may be supported by positive fundamental catalysts, increasing the likelihood of a successful trade. Similarly, strong fundamentals may reinforce bullish or bearish technical patterns, providing additional conviction for traders to enter or exit positions. By cross-referencing technical and fundamental factors, traders can increase the reliability and robustness of their trading decisions.

3. Risk Management:

Integrating technical and fundamental analysis helps traders manage risk effectively by providing multiple layers of analysis and validation. By considering both technical and fundamental factors, traders can identify potential risks and opportunities associated with a trade and adjust their risk management strategies accordingly. For example, strong fundamental factors may outweigh technical signals in high-conviction trades, while conflicting technical and fundamental signals may warrant caution and tighter risk controls.

Practical Strategies for Integrating Technical and Fundamental Analysis:

1. Conduct Multi-Timeframe Analysis:

Start by analyzing the long-term fundamentals and macroeconomic trends to establish a broader market outlook. Then, use technical analysis to identify short-term trends, patterns, and entry points within the broader market context. By conducting multi-timeframe analysis, traders can align their trades with both short-term technical setups and long-term fundamental trends.

2. Focus on Confluence Zones:

Look for confluence zones where technical and fundamental factors align to increase the probability of successful trades. For example, a technical support level coinciding with a key fundamental support level may present a strong buying opportunity. Similarly, a technical resistance level reinforced by negative fundamental catalysts may signal a potential shorting opportunity. By focusing on confluence zones, traders can capitalize on high-probability setups with multiple layers of confirmation.

3. Stay Informed:

Stay informed about market news, economic events, and corporate developments that may impact asset prices. Keep abreast of key economic indicators, earnings reports, central bank announcements, and geopolitical events that could influence market sentiment and drive price movements. By staying informed, traders can anticipate market trends, react swiftly to changing conditions, and adjust their trading strategies accordingly.

4. Continuously Learn and Adapt:

Continuously seek to improve your understanding of technical and fundamental analysis and refine your trading approach based on feedback and experience. Experiment with different indicators, strategies, and tools to find what works best for you in different market conditions. Be open to learning from mistakes and adapting your approach as market dynamics evolve over time.

Integrating technical and fundamental analysis wisely is essential for success and profitability in trading. By combining both approaches, traders can gain a comprehensive understanding of market dynamics, validate trading signals, manage risk effectively, and capitalize on high-probability trading opportunities. By implementing practical strategies for integrating technical and fundamental analysis, traders can increase their chances of making informed decisions and achieving long-term success in trading.

The Blueprint for Success: Developing a Trading Plan and Sticking to It

In trading, success is not merely a result of chance or luck but rather the culmination of meticulous planning, disciplined execution, and unwavering commitment to a well-defined trading plan. A trading plan serves as a roadmap, guiding traders through the complexities of the market and helping them navigate with clarity and purpose.

The Importance of a Trading Plan:

1. Clarity and Direction:

A trading plan provides traders with clarity and direction in their trading endeavors. By outlining specific goals, objectives, and strategies, a trading plan helps traders stay focused on what they aim to achieve in the markets. It serves as a blueprint for making informed decisions and navigating through the myriad of opportunities and challenges presented by the market.

2. Risk Management:

A trading plan incorporates risk management strategies to help traders protect their capital and minimize losses. By establishing risk parameters, such as stop-loss levels, position sizing rules, and maximum drawdown limits, traders can effectively manage risk and preserve their trading capital. A well-thought-out trading plan ensures that risk is managed prudently and in accordance with the trader's risk tolerance and financial goals.

3. Emotional Discipline:

Trading can evoke a range of emotions, including greed, fear, and uncertainty, which can cloud judgment and lead to impulsive decision-making. A trading plan acts as a psychological anchor, helping traders stay disciplined and emotionally detached from their trades. By following a predefined set of rules and guidelines, traders can mitigate the influence of emotions and maintain objectivity in their trading approach.

Key Components of a Trading Plan:

1. Trading Goals and Objectives:

Clearly define your trading goals and objectives, including financial targets, performance benchmarks, and timeframe for achieving them. Set realistic and achievable goals that align with your risk tolerance, trading experience, and overall investment objectives.

2. Market Analysis and Strategy:

Conduct a thorough analysis of the market and identify trading opportunities based on technical, fundamental, or sentiment analysis. Define your trading strategy, including entry and exit criteria, trade setup parameters, and risk management rules. Choose a trading style that suits your personality, preferences, and time constraints, whether it be day trading, swing trading, or long-term investing.

3. Risk Management Plan:

Develop a comprehensive risk management plan that outlines how you will manage risk in your trading activities. Determine your maximum risk per trade, position sizing rules, stop-loss placement strategies, and overall risk tolerance. Incorporate risk management tools and techniques to protect your capital and minimize losses in adverse market conditions.

4. Trade Execution and Management:

Specify how you will execute and manage your trades, including trade entry methods, order types, and trade monitoring procedures. Define your criteria for trade selection, including trade setup validation and confirmation signals. Establish guidelines for trade management, such as trailing stops, profit targets, and position scaling techniques.

Strategies for Sticking to Your Trading Plan:

1. Discipline and Consistency:

Cultivate discipline and consistency in your trading approach by adhering to your trading plan rigorously. Follow your predefined rules and guidelines consistently, regardless of market conditions or emotional impulses. Avoid making impulsive decisions or deviating from your plan based on fear, greed, or external influences.

2. Regular Review and Evaluation:

Review your trading plan regularly and evaluate its effectiveness in achieving your goals and objectives. Monitor your trading performance, identify areas for improvement, and adjust your plan accordingly. Continuously strive to refine and optimize your trading plan based on feedback and experience.

3. Accountability and Journaling:

Hold yourself accountable for adhering to your trading plan by maintaining a trading journal or log. Record details of each trade, including entry and exit points, rationale for the trade, and outcomes. Review your trading journal regularly to track your progress, identify patterns of behavior, and learn from mistakes. Use journaling as a tool for self-reflection and improvement in your trading journey.

4. Practice Patience and Resilience:

Trading success is not achieved overnight but rather through patience, resilience, and perseverance. Stay patient and resilient during periods of market volatility, drawdowns, or setbacks. Trust in your trading plan and remain focused on your long-term goals, even in the face of temporary challenges or obstacles.

Developing a trading plan and sticking to it is essential for success and longevity in trading. A well-crafted trading plan provides traders with clarity, direction, and discipline in their trading endeavors. By incorporating key components such as trading goals, market analysis, risk management, and trade execution strategies, traders can navigate the complexities of the market with confidence and purpose. By staying disciplined, consistent, and accountable to their trading plan, traders can increase their chances of achieving their financial goals and realizing long-term success in trading.

Achieving Trading Mastery: The Power of Practicing Mindfulness and Emotional Regulation Techniques

Emotions can run high, leading to impulsive decisions, irrational behavior, and detrimental effects on trading performance. Practicing mindfulness and emotional regulation techniques is essential for traders to maintain clarity, focus, and discipline in their trading endeavors.

The Importance of Mindfulness and Emotional Regulation in Trading:

1. Maintaining Focus:

Mindfulness enables traders to stay present and focused on the task at hand, despite the distractions and fluctuations of the market. By cultivating awareness of their thoughts, emotions, and physical sensations, traders can maintain clarity of mind and make informed decisions based on rational analysis rather than impulsive reactions.

2. Managing Emotions:

Emotional regulation techniques empower traders to manage their emotions effectively and prevent them from interfering with their trading decisions. By recognizing and acknowledging their emotions without judgment, traders can respond to market events with composure and objectivity, rather than succumbing to fear, greed, or anxiety.

3. Enhancing Discipline:

Mindfulness and emotional regulation foster discipline in trading by promoting self-awareness, self-control, and self-regulation. Traders who practice mindfulness are better equipped to adhere to their trading plans, follow predefined rules and guidelines, and resist the temptation to deviate from their strategies based on emotional impulses.

Key Techniques for Practicing Mindfulness and Emotional Regulation:

1. Breath Awareness:

Practice mindful breathing exercises to anchor yourself in the present moment and calm the mind. Focus your attention on the sensation of your breath as it enters and exits your body, allowing thoughts and emotions to arise and pass without attachment or judgment.

2. Body Scan Meditation:

Perform a body scan meditation to cultivate awareness of physical sensations and release tension or stress held in the body. Start at the top of your head and systematically move your attention down through each part of your body, noticing any areas of tightness, discomfort, or relaxation.

3. Thought Observation:

Practice observing your thoughts without getting caught up in them or reacting impulsively. Treat your thoughts like passing clouds in the sky, allowing them to come and go without attachment or identification. Notice any patterns or recurring themes in your thoughts related to trading and gently redirect your focus back to the present moment.

4. Emotional Labeling:

Label and acknowledge your emotions as they arise during trading. Use descriptive terms to identify and express your emotions, such as "I am feeling anxious about this trade" or "I am experiencing excitement after a profitable trade." By naming your emotions, you create distance between yourself and the emotion, allowing you to respond more skillfully rather than reactively.

Practical Strategies for Integrating Mindfulness and Emotional Regulation into Trading:

1. Establish a Mindfulness Routine:

Incorporate mindfulness practices into your daily routine to cultivate a sense of calm, clarity, and balance. Set aside time each day for meditation, breathing exercises, or mindful movement practices such as yoga or tai chi. Consistency is key to reaping the benefits of mindfulness over time.

2. Take Mindful Breaks:

Take regular breaks from trading to practice mindfulness and reset your mind between trades. Step away from your computer screen, close your eyes, and take a few deep breaths to center yourself. Use this time to check in with your thoughts and emotions, release any tension or stress, and return to trading with renewed focus and clarity.

3. Use Mindfulness as a Trading Tool:

Apply mindfulness techniques directly to your trading activities to enhance decision-making and performance. Before entering a trade, take a moment to pause and check in with yourself. Notice any emotions or thoughts that arise and assess whether they are influencing your decision. Use mindfulness to stay present and focused during the trade, observing market movements with curiosity and openness.

4. Practice Self-Compassion:

Be kind and compassionate with yourself as you navigate the ups and downs of trading. Recognize that losses and mistakes are a natural part of the learning process and an opportunity for growth and improvement. Cultivate self-compassion by treating yourself with the same kindness and understanding that you would offer to a friend facing similar challenges.

Practicing mindfulness and emotional regulation techniques is essential for success and well-being in trading. By cultivating awareness, managing emotions, and fostering discipline, traders can navigate the complexities of the market with clarity, composure, and confidence. By integrating mindfulness practices into their trading routine and applying emotional regulation techniques to their decision-making process, traders can increase their resilience, optimize performance, and achieve mastery in the art of trading.

The Path to Mastery: Learning from Mistakes and Adapting Your Trading Strategies

Success is often accompanied by a series of setbacks, failures, and learning experiences. While mistakes may be inevitable, it is how traders respond to these challenges that ultimately determines their growth and success in the market. Learning from mistakes and adapting trading strategies accordingly is a cornerstone of continuous improvement and mastery in trading.

Embracing Failure as a Learning Opportunity:

1. Shift in Perspective:

Instead of viewing failure as a setback or a reflection of personal inadequacy, embrace it as a valuable learning opportunity and an essential stepping stone on the path to success. Adopting a growth mindset allows traders to approach challenges with resilience, curiosity, and a willingness to learn and adapt.

2. Extracting Lessons:

Take time to reflect on your trading mistakes and identify key lessons to be learned from each experience. Analyze the factors that led to the mistake, whether it be a lapse in judgment, emotional decision-making, or flawed analysis. Use each mistake as a source of valuable feedback to refine your approach and improve your trading skills.

3. Iterative Improvement:

Recognize that trading success is a journey of continuous improvement and refinement. Treat each mistake as an opportunity to iterate and evolve your trading strategies, methods, and mindset. Embrace a process-oriented approach to trading, focusing on incremental progress and learning from both successes and failures along the way.

Key Lessons to Glean from Mistakes:

1. Risk Management:

Assess whether the mistake was related to inadequate risk management practices, such as failure to set appropriate stop-loss levels, over-leveraging, or insufficient position sizing. Recognize the importance of preserving capital and managing risk effectively to protect against significant losses and sustain long-term success in trading.

2. Emotional Discipline:

Reflect on how emotions may have influenced your decision-making process and contributed to the mistake. Identify common emotional triggers such as fear, greed, or impatience, and develop strategies for managing emotions more effectively. Cultivate emotional discipline by practicing mindfulness, self-awareness, and resilience in the face of adversity.

3. Trading Psychology:

Explore the psychological factors underlying the mistake, such as cognitive biases, irrational beliefs, or behavioral patterns. Investigate whether cognitive biases such as confirmation bias, overconfidence, or recency bias may have distorted your perception or judgment. Develop strategies for mitigating cognitive biases and fostering a more rational and objective approach to trading.

Practical Strategies for Adapting Trading Strategies:

1. Review and Revise:

Conduct a thorough review of your trading strategies, methods, and systems in light of the lessons learned from your mistakes. Identify areas for improvement and refinement, whether it be in your entry and exit criteria, trade management techniques, or risk management practices. Revise your trading plan accordingly to integrate new insights and adjustments.

2. Backtesting and Simulation:

Backtest your revised trading strategies using historical data to assess their performance and efficacy under various market conditions. Use simulation tools or paper trading to test your strategies in real-time without risking actual capital. Analyze the results and iterate on your strategies based on the feedback and insights gained from testing.

3. Continuous Learning:

Commit to ongoing education and skill development to stay informed about the latest market trends, strategies, and best practices. Attend trading seminars, webinars, or workshops to learn from experienced traders and industry experts. Read trading books, articles, and research papers to expand your knowledge and deepen your understanding of the markets.

4. Stay Flexible and Adaptive:

Remain flexible and adaptive in your approach to trading, recognizing that the markets are constantly evolving and dynamic. Be willing to adjust your strategies in response to changing market conditions, emerging trends, or new information. Maintain an open mind and a willingness to experiment with different approaches to find what works best for you.

Learning from mistakes and adapting trading strategies is essential for growth, resilience, and long-term success in trading. By embracing failure as a learning opportunity, extracting valuable lessons, and applying them to refine and improve your trading approach, you can navigate the challenges of the market with confidence and competence. By cultivating a growth mindset, staying committed to continuous learning, and remaining flexible and adaptive in your trading strategies, you can achieve mastery and achieve your financial goals in the world of trading.

Chapter 6: Maintaining Mental and Emotional Well-Being

The Trader's Wellness: Prioritizing Self-Care and Stress Management

Prioritizing self-care and stress management is paramount for maintaining overall well-being, sustaining peak performance, and achieving long-term success. While the pursuit of financial goals and market mastery may dominate traders' attention, neglecting self-care can lead to burnout, diminished mental health, and suboptimal trading outcomes.

The Importance of Prioritizing Self-Care:

1. Mental Health and Well-being:

Self-care is essential for safeguarding mental health and well-being in the high-pressure environment of trading. Engaging in self-care activities such as relaxation techniques, mindfulness practices, and leisure activities helps reduce stress, anxiety, and depression, fostering a positive mindset and emotional resilience.

2. Performance Optimization:

Prioritizing self-care enhances cognitive function, concentration, and decision-making abilities, leading to improved trading performance. Taking breaks, getting adequate rest, and maintaining a healthy work-life balance are essential for sustaining focus, productivity, and creativity in trading activities.

3. Longevity and Sustainability:

Sustainable success in trading requires a holistic approach that prioritizes physical, mental, and emotional health. Neglecting self-care can lead to burnout, fatigue, and decreased motivation, jeopardizing long-term sustainability and enjoyment in the trading profession. By prioritizing self-care, traders can maintain their health, vitality, and passion for trading over the long term.

Key Strategies for Managing Stress:

1. Stress Awareness:

Develop self-awareness of your stress triggers, symptoms, and responses to stress. Notice physical signs of stress such as muscle tension, headaches, or changes in appetite, as well as emotional signs such as irritability, mood swings, or difficulty concentrating. Awareness is the first step toward effectively managing stress and implementing appropriate coping strategies.

2. Stress Reduction Techniques:

Incorporate stress reduction techniques into your daily routine to promote relaxation and emotional well-being. Practice deep breathing exercises, progressive muscle relaxation, or guided imagery to calm the mind and body. Engage in activities that bring joy and fulfillment, such as spending time in nature, listening to music, or pursuing hobbies outside of trading.

3. Time Management and Boundaries:

Establish clear boundaries between work and personal life to prevent burnout and overwhelm. Allocate dedicated time for trading activities, but also prioritize time for rest, relaxation, and social connection. Practice effective time management techniques such as setting priorities, delegating tasks, and avoiding multitasking to reduce stress and increase productivity.

4. Healthy Lifestyle Choices:

Adopt a healthy lifestyle that supports overall well-being and resilience to stress. Prioritize regular physical activity, nutritious eating habits, and sufficient sleep to maintain energy levels, mental clarity, and emotional balance. Avoid excessive caffeine, alcohol, or stimulants that can exacerbate stress and disrupt sleep patterns.

Practical Tips for Incorporating Self-Care Practices:

1. Create a Self-Care Routine:

Develop a daily self-care routine that includes activities to nourish your body, mind, and spirit. Schedule time each day for self-care practices such as exercise, meditation, journaling, or relaxation techniques. Consistency is key to reaping the benefits of self-care and maintaining balance in your life.

2. Take Regular Breaks:

Incorporate short breaks into your trading routine to rest, recharge, and refocus your mind. Step away from your computer screen, stretch your body, and take deep breaths to alleviate tension and stress. Use break times to engage in activities that promote relaxation and rejuvenation, such as going for a walk, practicing mindfulness, or listening to calming music.

3. Seek Support:

Reach out to friends, family members, or fellow traders for support and encouragement during times of stress or difficulty. Join trading communities, forums, or support groups where you can connect with like-minded individuals, share experiences, and receive guidance and advice. Don't hesitate to seek professional help from a therapist, counselor, or mental health professional if needed.

4. Practice Gratitude:

Cultivate an attitude of gratitude by focusing on the positive aspects of your life and trading journey. Take time each day to reflect on things you are grateful for, whether it be small victories, supportive relationships, or opportunities for growth. Gratitude helps shift your perspective from scarcity to abundance, fostering resilience and emotional well-being.

Prioritizing self-care and stress management is essential for maintaining health, happiness, and success in the challenging and dynamic world of trading. By adopting healthy lifestyle habits, practicing stress reduction techniques, and incorporating self-care practices into your daily routine, you can enhance your overall well-being, sustain peak performance, and thrive in both your personal and professional life. Remember that self-care is not a luxury but a necessity for long-term success and fulfillment in the trading profession.

Achieving Harmony: Finding a Healthy Work-Life Balance in the Trading World

In the fast-paced and demanding realm of trading, finding a healthy work-life balance is essential for sustaining well-being, maximizing productivity, and achieving long-term success. The allure of financial gains and market opportunities can often lead traders to prioritize work at the expense of their personal lives, leading to burnout, stress, and diminished quality of life.

The Importance of a Healthy Work-Life Balance:

1. Well-being and Happiness:

A healthy work-life balance is crucial for maintaining physical health, mental well-being, and emotional resilience. Balancing work commitments with personal pursuits, leisure activities, and social connections promotes overall happiness, satisfaction, and fulfillment in life.

2. Productivity and Performance:

Finding equilibrium between work and personal life enhances productivity, creativity, and job satisfaction. Taking time to recharge, rest, and engage in non-work-related activities revitalizes the mind and body, leading to improved focus, concentration, and performance in trading activities.

3. Relationships and Connection:

Nurturing relationships with family members, friends, and loved ones is essential for building meaningful connections and fostering a sense of belonging and support. Investing time and energy in personal relationships strengthens social bonds, reduces feelings of isolation, and enhances overall life satisfaction.

Key Strategies for Achieving Work-Life Balance:

1. Establish Boundaries:

Set clear boundaries between work and personal life to prevent work from encroaching on your leisure time and vice versa. Define specific work hours and allocate dedicated time for personal activities, hobbies, and relaxation. Communicate your boundaries to colleagues, clients, and family members to ensure respect for your time and priorities.

2. Prioritize Self-Care:

Make self-care a priority by incorporating activities that promote physical, mental, and emotional well-being into your daily routine. Schedule time for exercise, relaxation, mindfulness practices, and hobbies that bring you joy and fulfillment. Taking care of yourself is essential for replenishing energy, reducing stress, and maintaining balance in your life.

3. Manage Time Effectively:

Practice effective time management techniques to optimize productivity and balance competing priorities. Prioritize tasks based on importance and urgency, delegate responsibilities when possible, and avoid procrastination and multitasking. Use tools such as calendars, planners, and to-do lists to organize your schedule and stay on track with your goals.

4. Delegate and Outsource:

Delegate tasks and responsibilities that can be performed by others to free up time for activities that are more meaningful or enjoyable. Whether it be hiring a virtual assistant, outsourcing administrative tasks, or leveraging automation tools, delegating allows you to focus on high-value activities and reduce overwhelm.

Practical Tips for Integrating Work and Life Harmoniously:

1. Create a Schedule:

Develop a balanced schedule that includes time for work, personal activities, relaxation, and socializing. Block out specific time slots for each activity and stick to your schedule as much as possible. Be flexible and open to adjustments as needed to accommodate changing priorities and commitments.

2. Practice Mindfulness:

Cultivate mindfulness in your daily life by staying present and attentive to the moment. Incorporate mindfulness practices such as meditation, deep breathing, or mindful walking into your routine to reduce stress, increase awareness, and promote a sense of calm and clarity.

3. Set Technology Boundaries:

Limit your exposure to digital devices and technology outside of work hours to minimize distractions and promote work-life balance. Establish tech-free zones or designated times for checking emails, messages, and notifications to prevent constant connectivity and allow for uninterrupted relaxation and downtime.

4. Invest in Relationships:

Prioritize quality time with family members, friends, and loved ones to nurture relationships and strengthen social connections. Schedule regular activities, outings, or gatherings to bond and create lasting memories together. Make an effort to be fully present and engaged during these interactions to deepen connections and foster intimacy.

Finding a healthy work-life balance is essential for well-being, productivity, and fulfillment in the trading world. By prioritizing self-care, establishing boundaries, managing time effectively, and investing in relationships, traders can achieve harmony between their professional and personal lives. Remember that work-life balance is a dynamic and ongoing process that requires conscious effort, flexibility, and adaptability. By adopting a holistic approach to life and embracing balance, traders can enjoy sustainable success and happiness in both their careers and personal lives.

The Power of Connection: Seeking Support from Peers and Mentors in Trading

In the dynamic and often solitary world of trading, seeking support from peers and mentors can be a game-changer. Whether you're a novice trader navigating the complexities of the market or an experienced professional looking to refine your skills, connecting with others in the trading community can provide invaluable insights, guidance, and camaraderie.

The Importance of Seeking Support:

1. Knowledge Sharing:

Peers and mentors can offer valuable knowledge, expertise, and perspectives gleaned from their own experiences in the market. By sharing insights, strategies, and lessons learned, they can help you expand your understanding of trading principles, techniques, and market dynamics.

2. Emotional Support:

Trading can be a mentally and emotionally challenging endeavor, fraught with uncertainty, stress, and self-doubt. Peers and mentors provide emotional support, encouragement, and empathy during times of difficulty or setbacks. They offer a listening ear, reassurance, and perspective to help you navigate the highs and lows of trading with resilience and confidence.

3. Accountability and Motivation:

Peers and mentors hold you accountable to your goals, commitments, and trading plans. They provide motivation, inspiration, and constructive feedback to keep you on track and focused on your objectives. Knowing that you have a supportive network of peers and mentors behind you can boost your confidence, discipline, and determination to succeed in trading.

Benefits of Seeking Support from Peers and Mentors:

1. Accelerated Learning:

Connecting with peers and mentors allows you to leverage their knowledge, expertise, and experience to accelerate your learning curve in trading. By tapping into their insights and guidance, you can avoid common pitfalls, learn from their mistakes, and gain a deeper understanding of effective trading strategies and techniques.

2. Expanded Network:

Building relationships with peers and mentors expands your network within the trading community, opening doors to new opportunities, collaborations, and partnerships. Networking with like-minded individuals allows you to exchange ideas, share resources, and collaborate on projects that can enhance your trading success and professional growth.

3. Personal Growth:

Interacting with peers and mentors fosters personal growth, self-awareness, and development in trading and beyond. They challenge your assumptions, broaden your perspectives, and push you outside your comfort zone to explore new possibilities and unleash your full potential as a trader and as an individual.

Practical Tips for Seeking Support from Peers and Mentors:

1. Join Trading Communities:

Participate in online forums, social media groups, and trading communities where traders gather to share knowledge, discuss market trends, and offer support. Engage in conversations, ask questions, and contribute your insights to build rapport and establish connections with fellow traders.

2. Attend Trading Events:

Attend trading seminars, workshops, conferences, and meetups to network with peers, mentors, and industry professionals in person. Take advantage of opportunities to connect with speakers, presenters, and attendees to exchange ideas, seek advice, and forge meaningful relationships.

3. Find a Mentor:

Seek out experienced traders or industry experts who can serve as mentors and provide guidance, advice, and mentorship in your trading journey. Look for mentors who have a track record of success, align with your trading style and values, and are willing to invest their time and expertise in your development.

4. Offer Value:

Build rapport and credibility with peers and mentors by offering value, support, and assistance in return. Share your knowledge, insights, and experiences generously, contribute to discussions and forums, and offer help or guidance to others whenever possible.

Seeking support from peers and mentors is a powerful strategy for enhancing your trading success, personal growth, and professional development. By connecting with others in the trading community, you can tap into a wealth of knowledge, experience, and support to accelerate your learning, navigate challenges, and achieve your goals in trading. Remember that building meaningful relationships takes time, effort, and genuine engagement, but the rewards of connection and collaboration in the trading world are well worth the investment.

The Art of Balance: Knowing When to Take Breaks and Step Away from Trading

Knowing when to take breaks and step away from the market is not only beneficial but essential for maintaining mental clarity, emotional well-being, and overall trading success. While the allure of constant market action and potential profits may tempt traders to stay glued to their screens for extended periods, neglecting the need for breaks can lead to burnout, decision fatigue, and diminished trading performance.

The Importance of Taking Breaks:

1. Mental Refreshment:

Taking breaks allows traders to recharge their mental batteries, clear their minds, and regain focus and concentration. Stepping away from the market for a brief period can help alleviate mental fatigue, enhance cognitive function, and improve decision-making abilities, leading to better trading performance.

2. Emotional Reset:

Breaks provide an opportunity for traders to manage their emotions, reduce stress, and maintain emotional balance in the face of market volatility and uncertainty. By stepping back from the intensity of trading, traders can gain perspective, regulate their emotions, and avoid making impulsive or emotionally-driven decisions.

3. Physical Well-being:

Sitting for prolonged periods in front of a computer screen can take a toll on physical health, leading to issues such as eye strain, back pain, and reduced circulation. Taking regular breaks allows traders to stretch, move their bodies, and engage in physical activities that promote blood flow, flexibility, and overall well-being.

Signs That It's Time to Take a Break:

1. Mental Fatigue:

Feeling mentally exhausted, unfocused, or unable to concentrate on trading activities is a clear indication that it's time to take a break. Mental fatigue can impair decision-making abilities and lead to suboptimal trading outcomes if not addressed promptly.

2. Emotional Distress:

Experiencing heightened emotions such as frustration, anxiety, or overwhelm while trading may signal the need for a break. Emotional distress can cloud judgment, trigger impulsive reactions, and increase the risk of making costly trading mistakes.

3. Physical Discomfort:

Physical symptoms such as eye strain, headaches, or muscle tension are warning signs that you may need to step away from your trading desk and give your body a break. Ignoring physical discomfort can exacerbate health issues and detract from overall trading performance.

Practical Strategies for Taking Breaks:

1. Schedule Regular Breaks:

Incorporate scheduled breaks into your trading routine to ensure consistent periods of rest and relaxation throughout the trading day. Set a timer or use trading platforms that offer built-in break reminders to prompt you to take regular pauses from trading activities.

2. Practice the Pomodoro Technique:

Adopt the Pomodoro Technique, a time management method that involves working in short bursts (typically 25 minutes) followed by a short break (5 minutes). Use a timer to divide your trading sessions into focused intervals of work and rest, allowing for optimal productivity and rejuvenation.

3. Engage in Mindful Activities:

Use breaks as an opportunity to engage in mindful activities that promote relaxation and stress relief. Practice deep breathing exercises, meditation, or mindfulness techniques to calm the mind, reduce tension, and restore balance.

4. Get Moving:

Take advantage of breaks to move your body and engage in physical activity. Stretch, go for a walk, or do some light exercise to improve circulation, boost energy levels, and counteract the sedentary nature of trading.

5. Disconnect from Screens:

Use breaks as a chance to disconnect from screens and technology to give your eyes and brain a break from constant stimulation. Step outside, enjoy nature, or engage in offline activities that allow you to rest and recharge away from the distractions of trading.

Knowing when to take breaks and step away from trading is essential for maintaining balance, well-being, and optimal performance in the market. By recognizing the signs of mental and emotional fatigue, and implementing practical strategies for taking breaks, traders can protect their health, preserve their sanity, and enhance their trading success in the long run. Remember that breaks are not a sign of weakness but a strategic tool for promoting productivity, creativity, and resilience in trading.

Chapter 7: Essential Insights for Succes in Trading

Mastering the Trading Mindset: Practical Strategies from "Trading in the Zone"

Trading in the financial markets is not solely about analyzing charts or following trading signals; it's also about mastering the psychological aspects of trading. In Mark Douglas' seminal work, "Trading in the Zone," traders are offered a blueprint for cultivating the right mindset and emotional discipline to navigate the challenges of the market successfully. Let's delve into practical strategies inspired by Douglas' insights that traders can implement to improve their trading performance.

1. Develop Self-Awareness:

Strategy: Start by cultivating self-awareness of your emotions, thought patterns, and behavioral tendencies while trading.

Implementation: Keep a trading journal to record your thoughts, emotions, and trading decisions. Reflect on past trades to identify patterns and areas for improvement.

2. Embrace Uncertainty:

Strategy: Accept that trading involves uncertainty and randomness, and focus on managing risk rather than predicting outcomes.

Implementation: Develop a robust risk management plan that includes setting stop-loss orders, managing position sizes, and diversifying your portfolio to mitigate risk.

3. Trade with Discipline:

Strategy: Stick to your trading plan and rules consistently, regardless of market conditions or emotions.

Implementation: Before entering a trade, define your entry and exit criteria, risk-reward ratio, and position size. Follow your plan rigorously and avoid deviating from it impulsively.

4. Cultivate Confidence:

Strategy: Build confidence in your trading abilities by focusing on process-oriented goals and continuous improvement.

Implementation: Set achievable goals such as following your trading plan, executing trades with discipline, and learning from mistakes. Celebrate small victories and milestones to boost confidence and motivation.

5. Practice Mindfulness:

Strategy: Stay present and focused on the current moment while trading, avoiding distractions and emotional reactions.

Implementation: Practice mindfulness techniques such as deep breathing, meditation, or visualization to calm the mind and maintain concentration during trading sessions.

6. Manage Emotions Effectively:

Strategy: Learn to recognize and manage common emotions such as fear, greed, and impatience that can influence trading decisions.

Implementation: Develop strategies for regulating emotions, such as taking breaks during periods of heightened stress, reframing negative thoughts, or using relaxation techniques to calm nerves.

7. Learn from Mistakes:

Strategy: View losses and mistakes as learning opportunities rather than failures, and use them to refine your trading approach.

Implementation: Analyze losing trades to identify what went wrong and how you can improve. Adjust your trading plan accordingly and apply the lessons learned to future trades.

8. Maintain Balance:

Strategy: Prioritize a healthy work-life balance to prevent burnout and maintain overall well-being.

Implementation: Schedule regular breaks during trading sessions to rest and recharge. Engage in activities outside of trading that bring joy and fulfillment, such as spending time with family, pursuing hobbies, or exercising.

By implementing these practical strategies inspired by "Trading in the Zone," traders can cultivate the right mindset and emotional discipline to succeed in the challenging and dynamic world of trading. Remember that mastering the trading mindset is an ongoing journey that requires patience, practice, and self-awareness. By committing to continuous improvement and adopting a disciplined approach to trading, traders can position themselves for long-term success and profitability in the market.

Unleashing Your Trading Potential: Practical Insights from "The Psychology of Trading"

"The Psychology of Trading" by Brett N. Steenbarger offers traders a comprehensive understanding of the psychological dynamics at play in the markets and provides actionable strategies for enhancing trading performance. Let's explore practical insights from the book and strategies that traders can implement to harness their trading potential.

1. Develop Emotional Intelligence:

Strategy: Cultivate emotional intelligence to recognize and manage emotions effectively while trading.

Implementation: Practice emotional awareness by identifying the emotions you experience during trading. Develop techniques such as mindfulness, journaling, or cognitive reframing to regulate emotions and maintain composure.

2. Set Clear Goals:

Strategy: Establish clear, measurable goals for your trading endeavors to provide direction and motivation.

Implementation: Define short-term and long-term goals that align with your trading objectives. Break down larger goals into smaller, achievable milestones and track your progress regularly.

3. Analyze Market Patterns:

Strategy: Use behavioral finance principles to analyze market patterns and understand the psychology of market participants.

Implementation: Study market trends, patterns, and investor sentiment to identify potential trading opportunities. Apply insights from behavioral finance theories to anticipate market movements and make informed trading decisions.

4. Engage in Deliberate Practice:

Strategy: Engage in deliberate practice to hone your trading skills and develop expertise over time.

Implementation: Identify specific areas of your trading that require improvement and design practice exercises to target those areas. Practice executing trades, analyzing charts, and managing risk in simulated or real-time trading environments.

5. Build Resilience:

Strategy: Develop resilience to cope with setbacks, losses, and challenges encountered in trading.

Implementation: Cultivate a growth mindset by viewing failures as opportunities for learning and growth. Develop coping strategies such as positive self-talk, seeking support from peers or mentors, and maintaining perspective during difficult times.

6. Foster Continuous Learning:

Strategy: Commit to lifelong learning and professional development to stay updated on market trends and trading strategies.

Implementation: Stay informed about market news, economic indicators, and industry developments through reputable sources. Invest in trading education, attend workshops or seminars, and engage with trading communities to exchange ideas and insights.

7. Practice Risk Management:

Strategy: Prioritize risk management to protect capital and preserve trading longevity.

Implementation: Set predefined risk parameters for each trade, including stop-loss orders, position sizing, and risk-reward ratios. Adhere to strict risk management rules and avoid overleveraging or taking excessive risks.

8. Foster a Supportive Environment:

Strategy: Surround yourself with a supportive network of peers, mentors, and trading communities to share experiences and insights.

Implementation: Participate in trading forums, social media groups, or local meetups to connect with other traders. Seek guidance and mentorship from experienced traders and offer support to fellow traders in return.

By incorporating these practical insights and strategies from "The Psychology of Trading" into your trading approach, you can enhance your psychological resilience, decision-making skills, and overall trading performance. Remember that successful trading requires a combination of technical expertise, psychological discipline, and continuous self-improvement. By investing in your psychological well-being and trading education, you can unlock your full trading potential and achieve long-term success in the markets.

Harnessing Market Psychology: Practical Tips from "Market Mind Games"

"Market Mind Games" by Denise Shull offers traders a unique perspective on market psychology, drawing insights from neuroscience and psychotherapy to decode the intricacies of investor behavior. Let's explore practical tips from the book and strategies that traders can implement to leverage market psychology effectively.

1. Understand Emotional Triggers:

Strategy: Develop an understanding of the emotional triggers that influence market participants' behavior and decision-making.

Implementation: Study market sentiment indicators, news headlines, and social media chatter to gauge investor emotions such as fear, greed, and optimism. Use this information to anticipate market movements and identify contrarian trading opportunities.

2. Practice Introspection:

Strategy: Engage in introspection to identify your own emotional biases and psychological tendencies that may impact your trading decisions.

Implementation: Reflect on past trading experiences and examine your emotional responses to different market scenarios. Identify patterns of behavior or cognitive biases that may hinder your trading performance and develop strategies to mitigate them.

3. Use Visualization Techniques:

Strategy: Harness the power of visualization techniques to enhance your trading performance and overcome psychological barriers.

Implementation: Visualize successful trading outcomes, confident decision-making, and optimal risk management strategies. Practice visualization exercises regularly to reinforce positive mental imagery and build self-confidence.

4. Leverage Pattern Recognition:

Strategy: Utilize pattern recognition skills to identify recurring market patterns and anticipate potential price movements.

Implementation: Study historical price charts and patterns to identify trends, support and resistance levels, and chart formations. Use technical analysis tools and indicators to confirm patterns and make informed trading decisions.

5. Develop Resilience:

Strategy: Cultivate resilience to navigate the ups and downs of trading with grace and perseverance.

Implementation: Adopt a growth mindset and view setbacks as opportunities for learning and growth. Develop coping strategies such as positive self-talk, stress management techniques, and maintaining a healthy work-life balance to stay resilient during challenging market conditions.

6. Practice Empathy:

Strategy: Cultivate empathy to better understand the motivations and perspectives of other market participants.

Implementation: Put yourself in the shoes of other traders and investors to empathize with their emotions, beliefs, and decision-making processes. Consider how market sentiment and collective psychology may influence price movements and market dynamics.

7. Manage Expectations:

Strategy: Set realistic expectations for your trading performance and outcomes to avoid disappointment and frustration.

Implementation: Establish achievable goals and benchmarks for your trading success, taking into account factors such as market volatility, risk tolerance, and trading experience. Focus on continuous improvement and progress rather than perfection.

8. Seek Feedback and Support:

Strategy: Seek feedback and support from peers, mentors, and trading communities to gain insights and perspectives on your trading approach.

Implementation: Participate in trading forums, online communities, or mastermind groups to share experiences, exchange ideas, and receive constructive feedback from fellow traders. Engage in ongoing learning and professional development to enhance your trading skills and knowledge.

By incorporating these practical tips and strategies from "Market Mind Games" into your trading routine, you can develop a deeper understanding of market psychology and improve your trading performance. Remember that successful trading is not just about analyzing charts and data; it's also about mastering your emotions, mindset, and psychological resilience. By leveraging insights from market psychology, you can gain a competitive edge in the markets and achieve long-term success as a trader.

Unlocking Trading Mastery: Practical Insights from "The Daily Trading Coach"

"The Daily Trading Coach" by Brett N. Steenbarger provides traders with a wealth of practical insights and exercises to enhance their trading skills and mindset. Let's explore some of the key strategies from the book and practical tips that traders can implement to unlock their trading mastery.

1. Set Clear Goals and Intentions:

Strategy: Define clear, specific goals and intentions for your trading journey to provide direction and motivation.

Implementation: Write down your trading goals, breaking them down into actionable steps and timelines. Review your goals regularly and adjust them as needed to stay aligned with your evolving trading objectives.

2. Commit to Continuous Learning:

Strategy: Embrace a mindset of continuous learning and professional development to stay updated on market trends and trading techniques.

Implementation: Dedicate time each day to learning and improving your trading skills. Read books, articles, and research papers on trading psychology, technical analysis, and market dynamics. Attend webinars, seminars, or workshops to expand your knowledge base and stay informed about industry developments.

3. Practice Deliberate Reflection:

Strategy: Engage in deliberate reflection to assess your trading performance, identify areas for improvement, and refine your trading approach.

Implementation: Set aside time each day to review your trades, analyzing both successful and unsuccessful outcomes. Reflect on your decision-making process, emotional reactions, and adherence to your trading plan. Identify patterns, strengths, and weaknesses to inform your future trading decisions.

4. Cultivate Discipline and Consistency:

Strategy: Develop discipline and consistency in your trading routine to maintain focus, execute trades with precision, and manage risk effectively.

Implementation: Establish a structured daily routine for your trading activities, including pre-market preparation, trading hours, and post-market analysis. Stick to your trading plan and rules consistently, avoiding impulsive decisions or deviations from your strategy.

5. Manage Emotional Resilience:

Strategy: Build emotional resilience to cope with the psychological challenges and uncertainties of trading.

Implementation: Practice stress management techniques such as deep breathing, visualization, or meditation to stay calm and focused during volatile market conditions. Develop coping strategies for dealing with losses, setbacks, and emotional triggers to maintain mental resilience and composure.

6. Seek Feedback and Accountability:

Strategy: Seek feedback and accountability from peers, mentors, or trading coaches to gain insights and perspectives on your trading performance.

Implementation: Join trading communities, forums, or mastermind groups to connect with other traders and share experiences. Seek out mentors or trading coaches who can provide constructive feedback, guidance, and accountability to help you reach your trading goals.

7. Embrace Adaptability and Flexibility:

Strategy: Embrace adaptability and flexibility in your trading approach to respond effectively to changing market conditions and opportunities.

Implementation: Stay open-minded and willing to adjust your trading strategies and tactics based on evolving market dynamics, new information, or feedback from your trading journal. Continuously evaluate and refine your approach to stay ahead of the curve and capitalize on emerging trends.

8. Practice Self-Care and Well-Being:

Strategy: Prioritize self-care and well-being to maintain physical health, mental clarity, and overall balance in your life.

Implementation: Incorporate regular exercise, healthy eating, and adequate sleep into your daily routine to support your physical and mental well-being. Take breaks, pursue hobbies, and spend time with loved ones to recharge and rejuvenate outside of trading hours.

By implementing these practical insights and strategies from "The Daily Trading Coach" into your trading routine, you can cultivate the skills, mindset, and discipline needed to achieve mastery in the markets. Remember that trading is a journey of continuous learning and growth, and success is built on a foundation of consistent effort, self-awareness, and resilience. With dedication, perseverance, and a commitment to lifelong learning, you can unlock your full potential as a trader and achieve your financial goals.

Mastering the Market: Practical Guidance from "Trading Psychology 2.0"

"Trading Psychology 2.0" by Brett N. Steenbarger offers traders advanced insights into the psychological dimensions of trading and provides practical strategies for optimizing performance. Let's explore some of the key strategies from the book and practical tips that traders can implement to master the market.

1. Harness Cognitive Behavioral Techniques:

Strategy: Apply cognitive-behavioral techniques to identify and overcome limiting beliefs, cognitive biases, and negative thought patterns.

Implementation: Practice cognitive restructuring by challenging irrational beliefs and replacing them with more rational and empowering thoughts. Use techniques such as cognitive reframing, thought recording, and positive self-talk to cultivate a resilient and adaptive mindset.

2. Develop Mental Toughness:

Strategy: Cultivate mental toughness to withstand the psychological challenges and pressures of trading with grace and resilience.

Implementation: Build mental toughness through exposure to controlled adversity and challenge. Gradually increase your tolerance for discomfort, uncertainty, and risk by pushing your comfort zone and embracing discomfort as a catalyst for growth and learning.

3. Utilize Behavioral Finance Insights:

Strategy: Incorporate insights from behavioral finance to understand how cognitive biases and emotional biases influence market behavior and decision-making.

Implementation: Study behavioral finance theories such as prospect theory, loss aversion, and herding behavior to gain insights into investor psychology and market dynamics. Use this knowledge to anticipate market trends, identify opportunities, and manage risk effectively.

4. Practice Mindfulness Meditation:

Strategy: Integrate mindfulness meditation practices into your daily routine to cultivate present-moment awareness, focus, and emotional regulation.

Implementation: Dedicate time each day to mindfulness meditation practice, focusing on your breath, sensations, or present thoughts and emotions. Use mindfulness techniques to anchor yourself in the present moment, reduce stress, and enhance concentration during trading.

5. Foster Self-Reflection and Evaluation:

Strategy: Engage in regular self-reflection and evaluation to assess your trading performance, identify strengths and weaknesses, and refine your trading approach.

Implementation: Set aside time each week to review your trading journal, analyze past trades, and evaluate your decision-making process. Identify patterns, errors, and areas for improvement, and develop action plans to address them proactively.

6. Develop Adaptive Trading Strategies:

Strategy: Develop adaptive trading strategies that can flexibly respond to changing market conditions, volatility, and trends.

Implementation: Experiment with different trading strategies, timeframes, and market instruments to diversify your approach and adapt to evolving market dynamics. Stay agile and open-minded, willing to adjust your strategies based on real-time data, feedback, and market insights.

7. Foster a Growth Mindset:

Strategy: Cultivate a growth mindset that embraces challenges, setbacks, and failures as opportunities for learning and growth.

Implementation: Embrace a mindset of continuous improvement and resilience, viewing obstacles and setbacks as stepping stones to success rather than barriers. Focus on the process of learning and development, rather than fixating on short-term outcomes or results.

8. Seek Mentorship and Support:

Strategy: Seek mentorship, guidance, and support from experienced traders, coaches, or mentors to accelerate your learning and development.

Implementation: Find a mentor or coach who can provide personalized guidance, feedback, and accountability tailored to your individual needs and trading goals. Join trading communities, forums, or mastermind groups to connect with like-minded traders and share experiences and insights.

By implementing these practical strategies and insights from "Trading Psychology 2.0" into your trading routine, you can enhance your psychological resilience, decision-making skills, and overall trading performance. Remember that trading psychology is a journey of self-discovery and self-mastery, and success is built on a foundation of continuous learning, self-awareness, and adaptability. With dedication, persistence, and a commitment to growth, you can master the market and achieve your financial goals as a trader.

Navigating the Market Maze: Practical Wisdom from "Mind Over Markets"

"Mind Over Markets" by James F. Dalton, Eric T. Jones, and Robert B. Dalton offers traders valuable insights into market psychology and the dynamics of supply and demand. Let's explore some of the key strategies from the book and practical tips that traders can implement to navigate the market maze effectively.

1. Understand Market Dynamics:

Strategy: Develop a deep understanding of market dynamics, including the interplay between supply and demand, price discovery, and market structure.

Implementation: Study market profile analysis and volume profile techniques to gain insights into market participants' behavior, preferences, and intentions. Use this information to identify key support and resistance levels, areas of accumulation or distribution, and potential trade opportunities.

2. Practice Patience and Observation:

Strategy: Cultivate patience and observational skills to wait for high-probability trading setups and avoid impulsive or emotional reactions.

Implementation: Monitor market developments patiently, waiting for clear signals and confirmation before entering trades. Develop the discipline to observe market behavior objectively, without succumbing to FOMO (Fear of Missing Out) or FOLO (Fear of Losing Out) tendencies.

3. Utilize Auction Market Principles:

Strategy: Apply auction market principles to understand how prices are determined through the interaction of buyers and sellers in the marketplace.

Implementation: Study market auction theory and concepts such as market profile, value area, and fair value to analyze price action and market structure. Use auction market principles to identify areas of value, excess, and imbalance in the market and plan trades accordingly.

4. Embrace Market Structure Analysis:

Strategy: Embrace market structure analysis to identify trends, reversals, and trading opportunities based on the underlying market dynamics.

Implementation: Analyze market structure through the lens of price action, volume, and time to identify key market phases such as balance, imbalance, trend, and range. Use market structure analysis to anticipate potential price movements, set realistic expectations, and manage risk effectively.

5. Develop Trading Plans:

Strategy: Develop comprehensive trading plans that outline your trading objectives, strategies, risk management rules, and trade execution parameters.

Implementation: Create a trading plan that defines your trading style, preferred markets, timeframes, and risk tolerance. Specify entry and exit criteria, position sizing rules, and trade management strategies. Review and update your trading plan regularly to reflect changing market conditions and personal preferences.

6. Implement Risk Management:

Strategy: Implement robust risk management practices to protect capital, preserve trading longevity, and minimize losses during adverse market conditions.

Implementation: Set predefined risk limits for each trade, based on your account size, risk tolerance, and trading strategy. Use stop-loss orders, position sizing techniques, and portfolio diversification to manage risk effectively and avoid catastrophic losses.

7. Focus on Process, Not Outcome:

Strategy: Focus on the process of trading rather than fixating on short-term outcomes or results.

Implementation: Shift your focus from the outcome of individual trades to the quality of your trading process and decision-making. Evaluate your trades based on their adherence to your trading plan, execution quality, and risk management discipline, rather than solely on their profitability.

8. Stay Adaptive and Flexible:

Strategy: Stay adaptive and flexible in your trading approach to respond effectively to changing market conditions and evolving trends.

Implementation: Continuously monitor market developments, news events, and economic indicators to stay informed and adapt your trading strategies accordingly. Be willing to adjust your approach, tactics, and risk management techniques based on real-time data and feedback from the market.

By implementing these practical strategies and insights from "Mind Over Markets" into your trading routine, you can enhance your understanding of market psychology, improve your decision-making skills, and achieve greater consistency and profitability as a trader. Remember that trading is both an art and a science, and success requires a combination of technical expertise, psychological resilience, and adaptability. With dedication, discipline, and a commitment to continuous learning, you can navigate the market maze with confidence and achieve your trading goals.

Thriving in Trading: Practical Techniques from "Reminiscences of a Stock Operator"

"Reminiscences of a Stock Operator" by Edwin Lefèvre may not be explicitly focused on trading psychology, but it offers invaluable insights into market dynamics, trader mentality, and risk management. Let's explore some of the key strategies from the book and practical tips that traders can implement to thrive in their trading endeavors.

1. Embrace Market Realism:

Strategy: Embrace a realistic view of the markets, recognizing that they are driven by human psychology, emotions, and speculation.

Implementation: Study historical market cycles, bubbles, and crashes to understand the recurring patterns and behaviors of market participants. Develop a healthy skepticism towards market hype, irrational exuberance, and speculative manias.

2. Practice Independent Thinking:

Strategy: Cultivate independent thinking and critical analysis skills to form your own market opinions and trading decisions.

Implementation: Conduct thorough research and analysis using multiple sources of information and perspectives. Avoid herd mentality and groupthink, relying instead on your own judgment and analysis to guide your trading decisions.

3. Manage Risk Prudently:

Strategy: Implement prudent risk management practices to protect capital and preserve trading longevity.

Implementation: Set predefined risk limits for each trade and adhere to strict risk management rules. Use stop-loss orders, position sizing techniques, and diversification strategies to manage risk effectively and avoid catastrophic losses.

4. Adapt to Market Conditions:

Strategy: Stay adaptive and flexible in your trading approach to respond effectively to changing market conditions and trends.

Implementation: Monitor market developments, news events, and economic indicators to identify emerging opportunities and threats. Be willing to adjust your trading strategies, tactics, and risk management techniques based on real-time data and feedback from the market.

5. Learn from Experience:

Strategy: Learn from both successes and failures to refine your trading approach and improve your performance over time.

Implementation: Keep a detailed trading journal to record your trades, thoughts, emotions, and lessons learned. Review your journal regularly to identify patterns, mistakes, and areas for improvement. Use past experiences to inform your future trading decisions and refine your trading strategy.

6. Cultivate Psychological Resilience:

Strategy: Cultivate psychological resilience to cope with the emotional ups and downs of trading and maintain mental clarity and composure.

Implementation: Practice stress management techniques such as deep breathing, visualization, or meditation to stay calm and focused during volatile market conditions. Develop coping strategies for dealing with losses, setbacks, and emotional triggers to maintain mental resilience and discipline.

7. Focus on Process, Not Outcome:

Strategy: Focus on the process of trading rather than fixating on short-term outcomes or results.

Implementation: Evaluate your trades based on their adherence to your trading plan, execution quality, and risk management discipline, rather than solely on their profitability. Shift your focus from the outcome of individual trades to the quality of your trading process and decision-making.

8. Maintain Discipline and Patience:

Strategy: Maintain discipline and patience in your trading approach, avoiding impulsive or emotional reactions to market fluctuations.

Implementation: Stick to your trading plan and rules consistently, regardless of market conditions or emotions. Exercise patience and restraint, waiting for high-probability trading setups and avoiding the temptation to overtrade or chase after losses.

By implementing these practical techniques and insights from "Reminiscences of a Stock Operator" into your trading routine, you can enhance your understanding of market dynamics, improve your decision-making skills, and achieve greater consistency and profitability as a trader. Remember that trading is both an art and a science, and success requires a combination of technical expertise, psychological resilience, and discipline. With dedication, discipline, and a commitment to continuous learning, you can thrive in your trading endeavors and achieve your financial goals.

Conclusion

Throughout this ebook, we have explored a multitude of topics aimed at equipping traders with the tools and mindset necessary to navigate the challenges of the market and achieve sustainable success.

From understanding the importance of trading psychology and emotional regulation to implementing practical strategies for managing cognitive biases and cultivating patience and discipline, each chapter has delved into critical aspects of the trader's journey. We have explored the role of emotions such as fear, greed, and overconfidence in shaping trading decisions, as well as the detrimental impact of impulsive behavior, revenge trading, and chasing losses.

Moreover, we have discussed the significance of setting realistic goals and expectations, embracing failure as a learning opportunity, and prioritizing self-care and stress management to maintain a healthy work-life balance. We have highlighted the importance of seeking support from peers and mentors, recognizing when to take breaks and step away from trading, and implementing risk management techniques to protect capital and minimize losses.

Ultimately, achieving success in forex trading requires a combination of knowledge, skill, and mindset. It is not merely about making profitable trades but about developing resilience in the face of adversity, maintaining emotional equilibrium amid market fluctuations, and continuously evolving and adapting to changing conditions. By integrating the insights and strategies presented in this ebook into their trading approach, traders can cultivate the mindset and habits necessary to thrive in the competitive and dynamic world of forex trading.

As traders embark on their journey towards mastery, may they approach each trade with mindfulness, discipline, and self-awareness, recognizing that success is not defined by individual trades but by the consistency and integrity of their approach over time. With a commitment to continuous learning, self-improvement, and resilience, traders can navigate the highs and lows of the market with confidence, integrity, and a steadfast commitment to their financial goals.

www.ingramcontent.com/pod-product-compliance
Lightning Source LLC
Chambersburg PA
CBHW031744150726
47989CB00006B/2588